Practicing Sociology

Selected Fields

Robert A. Dentler

PRAEGER

Westport, Connecticut
London

Library of Congress Cataloging-in-Publication Data

Dentler, Robert A., 1928–
    Practicing sociology : selected fields / Robert A. Dentler.
        p. cm.
    Includes bibliographical references and index.
    ISBN 0–275–97515–0 (alk. paper)—ISBN 0–275–97516–9 (pbk. : alk. paper)
    1. Applied sociology.   2. Sociology—History.   3. Social change.   4. Social
problems.   I. Title.
HN29.5.D46   2002
301—dc21   2001036675

British Library Cataloguing in Publication Data is available.

Library of Congress Catalog Card Number: 2001036675
ISBN: 0–275–97515–0
        0–275–97516–9 (pbk.)

First published in 2002

Praeger Publishers, 88 Post Road West, Westport, CT 06881
An imprint of Greenwood Publishing Group, Inc.
www.praeger.com

Printed in the United States of America

The paper used in this book complies with the
Permanent Paper Standard issued by the National
Information Standards Organization (Z39.48–1984).

10   9   8   7   6   5   4   3   2   1

Contents

Preface

This book was written for sociologists and their students who are studying, teaching, or working in the fields of sociological practice, applied sociology, and clinical sociology. These three semantic labels float about on many college and university campuses today. Their definitions and boundaries are matters subject to debate. Any one or all three labels and areas may be subsumed within a single course or a series of courses within an academic major, or indeed an entire degree program. The labels are also tossed about and put to different uses today by government agencies, businesses, and human service agencies.

The American Sociological Association (ASA) *Directory of Programs in Applied Sociology and Practice* (Vaughn and Krause 1997) lists 123 sociology departments in the United States with verified undergraduate or graduate courses in applied sociology, clinical sociology, and sociological practice. Some offer just two or three courses, whereas others sponsor whole degree programs. The ASA *Guide to Graduate Departments* (1997) lists twenty additional sociology departments claiming special programs of study in applied sociology, evaluation research, or sociological practice. An estimated 24,000 graduate students have enrolled each school year in recent years in courses in which practice was the main feature of the agenda.

There are some journals that provide contemporary windows on the world of practice. They include the *Journal of Applied Sociology*; *Social Insights*; *Sociological Practice: A Journal of Clinical and Applied Sociology*, and the more narrowly specialized *American Journal of Evaluation*. At least two up-to-date books are available: *Solution-Centered Sociology: Addressing Problems through Applied Sociology* (Steele, Scarisbrick-Hauser, and Hauser 1999), and *Directions in Applied Sociology: Presidential Addresses of the Society for Applied Sociology* (Steele and Iutcovich 1997). The first of these is aimed at undergraduates; the second is a compendium of speeches, of which only a few are current. Other books are listed in the "References" section of this preface. However, they are narrowly tailored to fit a particular course (as with *Investigating the Social World* [Schutt 1999], a research methods text), or they are out of date or out of print or both.

There are also three professional associations within the United States devoted to these emerging fields. They are the Society for Applied Sociology, the Sociological Practice Association, and the Sociological Practice Section of the American Sociological Association. Each of these holds meetings, publishes newsletters, and works to disseminate knowledge about practice. They are small—each has between 400 and 600 members, about a quarter of whom are overlapping—and they have not succeeded in becoming the voice of the many thousands of sociologically educated men and women who do applied work in nonacademic settings all over the world. Sociologists coming out of university programs of study tend to lose their identification with the field as they become increasingly invested in a particular field of practice. Their numbers are very large but their professional affiliations increasingly tend to be with associations linked closely with their lines of work.

This book aims to foster the professional unit of the field of practice. It does not attempt to cover all of the diverse fields of practice; instead, it presents a number of those fields in considerable depth, along with a summary of the history of the evolution of practice and a chapter on intellectual resources from social theory often utilized to guide or ground practice today. The rest of this preface identifies fields of practice not covered in the main book and cites references to literature in each field.

Health care policies, programs, and practices constitute the single largest field within American applied sociology (Aiken and Mechanic 1986). Sociological practitioners do research on teams comprised of physicians, nurses, and allied health care professionals. Some work directly with patients in units of behavioral medicine in hospitals and rehabilitation centers. Sometimes termed *medical sociology* (Bird, Conrad, and Fremont 2000), this field has, since the late 1980s, commanded the largest amount of governmental and foundation funding.

Criminology, corrections, and sociological practice in all aspects of criminal justice constitute a large part of applied sociology. Criminology is reviewed regularly in the journal *Annual Review of Sociology*. Larson and Garrett (1996) provide a comprehensive view of this field, as does Stevens for the subfield of corrections (2000). Adler and Laufer (1993) make helpful connections between social theory and criminology, and a recent book of readings by Simpson (2000) illuminates the uses of sociology in interpreting criminality and criminal justice practices.

Community studies, planning, and development is a sturdy, long-standing field for the utilization of sociological knowledge. Phifer (1990) traces this field back into late nineteenth-century rural life in America. A good review of approaches to community intervention is provided by Hyman (1990). Cernea (1991) extends this tradition deep into investments in aid for foreign areas and related international areas.

Sociologists also practice as sociotherapists. This activity takes place primarily in the domain of clinical sociology. They work as therapists in counseling centers, hospitals, and community mental health centers, as well as individual practitioners. Swann laid a general knowledge basis for this field (1984), as did Fritz in the same period (1985). Darling covered the field most recently (2000).

I wrote this book for use in a course designed to orient incoming students in an M.A. program in applied sociology at the University of Massachusetts at Boston. This degree program began in 1983 and continues to flourish into these first months of the new century. In it, as in most similar programs around the nation, the nature and fundamentals of practice must be presented, as students come in from a great variety of jobs and from fields of study that include psychology, economics, and political science, as well as sociology.

ACKNOWLEDGMENTS

Jerrald Krause helped to conceptualize this book and to write a major portion of chapter 2. Colleagues Richard Robbins, Nelson Foote, Stephen Steele, Jay Weinstein, Carolyn Peelle, and Russell Schutt have offered encouragement and a zest for sociological practice that has inspired me. The following colleagues in the applied sociology graduate program at the University of Massachusetts at Boston—Richard Robbins, James Blackwell, Siamak Movahedi, Calvin Larson, Gerald Garrett, Bette Woody, and Richard Kronish—have shared the challenge of teaching over the past two decades. My graduate students have also contributed profoundly through their papers, seminar contributions, and theses.

I owe an older debt to my mentors, Ernest W. Burgess and Peter H. Rossi; to my co-author and colleague Philips Cutright; and to Charles V. Willie, for their stimulating guidance and exemplary performances as social scientists over many decades.

Special thanks are also due to Praeger Publishers editor Suzanne I. Staszak-Silva for her encouragement, patience, and high standards; and to Brooke Graves of Graves Editorial Service, for her superb editing of the text.

REFERENCES

Adler, F., and W. S. Laufer. 1993. *New Directions in Criminological Theory.* New Brunswick, N.J.: Transaction Publishers.

Aiken, L. H., and D. Mechanic. 1986. *Applications of Social Science to Clinical Medicine and Health Policy.* New Brunswick, N.J.: Rutgers University Press.

American Sociological Association. 1997. *Guide to Graduate Departments.* Washington, D.C.: American Sociological Association.

Bird, C. E., Peter Conrad, and A. M. Fremont, eds. 2000. *Handbook of Medical Sociology.* Upper Saddle River, N.J.: Prentice Hall.

Cernea, M. M., ed. 1991. *Putting People First: Sociological Variables in Rural Development.* New York: Oxford University Press [for the World Bank].

Darling, R. B. 2000. *Clinical Sociology.* Norwell, Calif.: Kluwer Academic Publishers.

Fritz, J. M. 1985. *The Clinical Sociology Handbook.* New York: Garland.

Hyman, D. 1990. Six models of community intervention: A dialectical synthesis of social theory and social action. *Sociological Practice* 8: 32–47.

Larson, C. J., and G. R. Garrett. 1996. *Crime, Justice, and Society.* Dix Hills, N.Y.: General Hall.

Phifer, B. M. 1990. Community development in America: A brief history. *Sociological Practice* 8: 18–31.

Schutt, R. K. 1999. *Investigating the Social World: The Process and Practice of Research.* 2d ed. Thousand Oaks, Calif.: Pine Forge Press.

Simpson, S., ed. 2000. *Of Crime and Criminality: The Use of Theory in Everyday Life.* Thousand Oaks, Calif.: Pine Forge Press.

Steele, S. F., and J. M. Iutcovich, eds. 1997. *Directions in Applied Sociology: Presidential Addresses of the Society for Applied Sociology.* Arnold, Md.: Society for Applied Sociology.

Steele, S. F., A. M. Scarisbrick-Hauser, and W. J. Hauser. 1999. *Solution-Centered Sociology: Addressing Problems through Applied Sociology.* Thousand Oaks, Calif.: Sage Publications.

Stevens, D. J., ed. 2000. *Corrections.* Bellvue, Wash.: Coursewise.

Swann, A. L. 1984. *The Practice of Clinical Sociology and Sociotherapy.* Cambridge, Mass.: Schenkman Publishing.

Vaughn, J., and J. Krause, eds., 1997. *Directory of Programs in Applied Sociology and Practice.* Washington, D.C.: American Sociological Association.

SUPPLEMENTAL READING

Stephens, W. R., Jr. 1999. *Careers in Sociology.* 2d ed. Boston: Allyn Bacon.

Strauss, R., ed. 1994. *Using Sociology.* Dix Hills, N.Y.: General Hall.

Sullivan, T. J. 1992. *Applied Sociology: Research and Critical Thinking.* New York: Macmillan.

1

The History of Sociological Practice

INTRODUCTION

This chapter presents the historical context and social movements that fostered the emergence of sociological practice. Abraham Lincoln observed that unless we know where we have been, we will not know where we are going. It is equally true that unless we know where we are today, history of the past will give us very little guidance to the future.

Present-day sociological practice was defined this way by Rodolfo Alvarez in 1991, at a session of the Section on Sociological Practice of the American Sociological Association: "Sociological practice is the development and use of social intervention techniques to precipitate social change beneficial to specific categories of participants within specific types of social systems" (cited in Olsen 1992). Marvin Olsen expanded on this definition, offering this alternative: "Sociological practice is the utilization of sociological knowledge to benefit society and social life through research, action, or administration" (1992, 50). The concern of this chapter is to provide an account of the periods in Western history from the eighteenth century to the present, with the aim of illuminating the specific context that informed and then led to increasingly professional formulations of sociological practice.

There are two good ways of identifying a field of knowledge and practice within that field. One is that the field itself tends to endure. It is inhabited over generations by the same species of preoccupying questions, although a few of these may, at least in the more exact sciences, come to be answered once and for all. The other is that those who work the field believe in the worth and validity of those questions and tend to see reality through the perspectives they learn from their work.

The field of sociology was not staked out until August Comte declared it a field and named it as such in the 1820s, although the questions this field would make its own had been discussed since antiquity in philosophy and theology. Neil Smelser summarized these neatly in his treatise on *Sociology* (1994, 4):

1. What are the major patterns of change and modernization that occur in societies?
2. Are there somewhat universal social or cultural mechanisms that trigger and speed forward or impede the process of societal change?
3. Social structures generate and maintain inequalities. How do these originate, and what are their functions and effects on human welfare?
4. As change gathers velocity, what holds societies and groups together?
5. How are change, resistance to change, and the cementing forces in the social structure mediated or governed by the main social institutions and associational subsystems?

OUR EIGHTEENTH-CENTURY ROOTS

These preoccupying questions, like all others in the history of ideas, evolved out of the theories and methods of inquiry common to intellectuals in the eighteenth century. The leading British and French philosophers—Hobbes, Locke, Hume, and Condillac, among many others—were struggling to account for the nature of society and the polity. To do so in the tradition of reason rather than religion, they had first to formulate theories about human nature, individual personality, and the processes of perception and cognition. Their methods were historical and philosophical, but their initial concerns were essentially psychological rather than sociological. Notions of the association of ideas, for example, and of the tendency of human nature to be brutish and only occasionally altruistic, were the rudiments of a naturalistic psychology. Other life sciences, notably biology and chemistry, were beginning to dominate thinking about human nature, and the millennium of theological assumptions about supernatural determination of all aspects of life and behavior began to draw to a close.

The methods of the eighteenth-century natural philosophers were those of historiography and systematic logic grounded in philosophy. Bernard and Bernard (1943) explained the approach of these thinkers to the analysis and improvement of society in this way: The first law of human society, said the philosophers, is that it is the product of culture—of accumulated thought ways and habits passed down across generations within particular environments. The second law is that human nature itself is a dynamic function of ever-changing environmental and economic conditions. One of the assumptions underlying the second law was that, with the tools of history and scientific reason, humankind could move gradually toward mastery of the environment and could bend the pattern of society toward unlimited progress.

Central to social thought during the Enlightenment, then, was the conviction that increased knowledge and understanding of society was the first requirement of intentional social progress. Perhaps the icon of sociological practice, the Marquis de Condorcet was the most eloquent philosopher of progress, the father of social planning, and the victim—by poisoning while under arrest, we suspect—of his great ideas about the perfectibility of the human condition.

Condorcet's *Sketch for a Historical Picture of the Progress of the Human Mind*, written while he was in hiding from the Jacobins, represents humans as evolving from savagery toward civility, social virtue, and happiness. His nine epochs of history formulate, for the first time in modern Western thought, a detailed naturalistic vision of societal evolution. The tenth epoch of the future, he reasoned, would eliminate inequality between nations and social classes, and would result in the optimization of intelligence, individual morality, and physical well-being. Condorcet's mightiest engine with which to pull us into his tenth epoch was, of course, education. His ideas made the discipline of sociology the science of societal and individual progress through knowledge and its cultural dissemination.

THE TREE OF SOCIOLOGY

The roots of sociology are thus embedded in the soil of the Enlightenment, when speculation and conceptualization about the natural philosophy of the human condition were first refined and modernized. The initial impulse toward improving the human condition was strong and shaped the self-conscious purposes of societal analysis, yet as Bernard and Bernard (1943, 29) noted,

Condorcet and Godwin were idealists and moralists who had ample opportunity to observe the suffering of the people. . . . Yet [they] were far from being concrete and detailed in their analysis of the social situations of the time or in their proposals for reform. . . . These men, even at their best . . . could not get down to a concrete analysis of society as it was.

The nineteenth century became the point where attention turned from the sweeping history of epochs to concrete analysis. A good symbol of this change is Charles Darwin's obsession with a collection of bird fossils he brought home with him, along with thousands of other specimens and samples, from his round-the-world voyage as a young naturalist aboard the H.M.S. *Beagle*. What he classified as wrens, finches, and blackbirds from three Galápagos islands were later reclassified (with the help of a colleague, John Gould) as a series of ground finches—in fact a group containing twelve species of finches within it. It was out of protracted examination and analysis of the details of this discovery that some of the first clues to natural selection within island habitats took shape. These clues, along with equally close analysis of thousands of other collections and with experiments on seeds and in the breeding of pigeons and peahens, eventually led to Darwin's *Origin of Species*. In the same era, between 1830 and 1850, Darwin and hundreds of naturalists like him became philosophical positivists as well.

The liberating power of empirical science—geology, botany, zoology, chemistry, and paleontology—became one of the defining features of the first half of the nineteenth century. Its handmaiden in all aspects of the emerging social sciences was the concrete analysis of social, economic, and psychological events.

Excitement about the mapping and description of contemporary societies, remote as well as immediate, paralleled excitement about geology, archeology, and field biology and botany. The curriculum of schools and colleges throughout the West were devoted to antiquity, classical studies, history of the distant past, and the practical arts of writing and rhetoric and mathematics. Gradually, however, the curriculum was augmented by increasingly analytical depictions of the current civilization.

Materials were hard to come by, however. The commentators and intellectuals of the first half of the nineteenth century were few indeed, and were concentrated within a few urban salons and great university centers. Nevertheless, the breaking news of the new sciences and industrial technologies was powerful enough to span the distance between cities, estates, and small villages. The spark jumped the gap between the small clusters of intellectuals and the rapidly multiplying associations—discussion groups, book clubs, forums, lecture clubs and circuits. As the associations took hold, moreover, they became imbued with the vision of social reform and social service in the support of progress. As Bernard and Bernard explain it (1943, 33), "Social Science . . . was not a generic term. . . . [I]t was the religion of a society in the throes of industrialization, just as theology had been the religion of the old feudal world."

There were individual social scientists who, like their counterparts in other disciplines, were professionalizing their concern with technical questions and with the formulation of researchable questions whose answers they would value for their own sake. This set of developments was small, however, compared to the rise of mass audiences for self-conscious inquiry into knowledge about contemporary life. The mass audiences imbued their interest with religious and moral zeal.

Viewing nature or the stars in a proper manner was regarded as a source of moral improvement. Henry David Thoreau and Ralph Waldo Emerson were naturalistic observers who were convinced that an accurate perception of reality would help lead humans toward a better life. Social wisdom is the encompassing theme of *Walden*. In any event, the first half of the nineteenth century was a time of explosive growth in the popularity and utilization of scientific thought, coupled with very strong notions that an empirically accurate and deep understanding of society and the human condition would generate great social progress.

COMTE AND THE ADVENT OF SOCIOLOGY

Auguste Comte (1798–1857), an independent scholar-genius studying in Paris, was the first person to synthesize the best ideas of the eighteenth-century political philosophers Condorcet, A.-R.-J. Turgot, and Joseph de Maistre with the best thinking of his friend and contemporary, Henri de Saint-Simon, a social reformer and one of the founders of socialism. Exceptionally and precociously gifted, Comte steeped himself in mathematics and science in adolescence. At the same time he wandered the streets of Paris, taking in the misery and chaos of a collapsing, postrevolutionary city, and dreamed of creating a political order that would reconstruct and improve conditions. His conduct was that of the universal urban radical. He repudiated the Roman Catholicism of his family, was expelled from college, joined youth and worker movements of the time in Paris, married a prostitute from the streets, and suffered from occasional bouts of suicidal depression. He was not an atheist; rather, he regarded God as part of a set of phenomena not amenable to positive philosophy, although in his later years he wrote *Positive Polity,* in which he invented a kind of religion, with rituals, for secular positivists. In his twenties, the decade when his garret life and street adventures were at their peak, Comte also read both voraciously and systematically and began his writings on positivism.

The times were ripe for synthesis, extension, and application of the ideas and ideals of the Age of Reason. Scientific approaches to all phenomena, events, and human behavior were gaining in popularity in every country from Russia to Germany to the United States. With few exceptions, colleges and universities remained occupied with humanistic and theological studies and with service to the emerging learned professions. Amateurism and independent scholarship enjoyed a field day. Comte made a part of his very meager livelihood delivering lectures to groups of unschooled laborers in Paris, for example. As mass literacy began to become reality, associations, societies, and intellectual gatherings of every kind became nearly as popular between 1820 and 1850 as the puppet theater and the local opera house.

Comte compressed Condorcet's many epochs of societies into three, and envisioned a fourth, emerging epoch in which *positive* knowledge—knowledge based upon naturalistic evidence, observation, and reason alone, unaided by divine inspiration or theological authority—would create and put into place the laws of society. (He actually formulated the first series of those laws.) These laws, in turn, would gradually generate a more perfect polity. Given the primacy for Comte of scientific knowledge, he also classified all existing sciences into a hierarchy that culminated in a pinnacle where sociology would reign as the queen of all sciences. Incidentally, Comte did not include psychology in his pyramid. Behaviorism based upon the science we now call neurology was advanced by Comte as wholly sufficient to account for observable differences in human actions. As Larson noted,

To Comte, the purpose of scientifically acquired knowledge of the laws of social order and change is to permit "prevision," or prediction. Prediction is regarded as prerequisite to the possibility of effective and accurate social planning and social engineering. When accurate prediction of complex societal events and activities becomes a reality, the rule of reason is presumed to be at hand and the human possibilities thereby unlimited. (1993, 3)

In one sense then, the idea of sociological practice was part of Auguste Comte's originating vision of our field of knowledge. In his distinction between "the statical of sociology" and "social dynamics" he worked to express the idea central to his vision: namely, that statics would identify and map the laws of society while dynamics would follow by utilizing the laws to engineer the future progress of society.

THE POST-COMTEIAN ERA

Herbert Spencer, a Derbyshire Englishman, was ten years old when Comte published *Positive Philosophy.* An early and voracious reader in the natural sciences, Spencer was self-taught—the next to the last, as we shall show, of the great amateurs who created sociology. He never attended college and he never held an academic post except for two years as a schoolteacher, yet his books and essays dominated social scientific and social philosophical thinking in England and America from 1850 to 1890.

His gifted imagination was first kindled by the idea of evolution. His notion of the evolution of biological species was, in fact, published earlier than Darwin's *Origin of Species,* and he was the first to coin the phrase "survival of the fittest." Although he occasionally emphasized that he was not a follower of Auguste Comte, he did embrace the proposition that all scientists are positivists—and he published *Social Statics* in 1851. His "organicism," derived from biology, was imitative of Comte as well.

Spencer, unlike Comte, lived a long and comfortable life during decades far less turbulent than those of the 1790s and the early 1800s. He worked as a journalist and magazine editor for about ten years, but retired after receiving an inheritance. His life was devoted to armchair study, writing, and conversations with the influential celebrities of his day. Spencer was a committed member of the Liberal Party, a party embracing the merits of an industrial society and economy whose workings, in the earlier notions of Adam Smith, were voluntary, rationalistic, and delicately balanced. He feared a time when liberals would verge upon social legislation that would, he said, create a kind of social slavery of citizens. Much of the conservatism of Margaret Thatcher,

Barry Goldwater, Ronald Reagan, and Newt Gingrich contains echoes of Spencerian ideals, although liberalism itself has been transmuted in the twentieth century.

To the mature Herbert Spencer, social engineering, social planning, and policy interventions—all at the core of sociological practice—were sources of contamination of the natural evolutionary process in society. Left unfettered and unmanipulated by parliaments, said Spencer, human society would evolve gradually toward true and complete individual liberty and responsibility.

Karl Heinrich Marx was born in 1818, just twelve years before the publication of Comte's *Positive Philosophy*. His father Heinrich, a lawyer, was a man of the Age of Reason, a devotee of Voltaire. Studying at the University of Berlin, young Karl was caught up in Hegelian philosophy. Although Hegel wrote from within the Christian theological tradition, student followers at Berlin in the late 1830s were moving toward revolutionary politics laced with atheism. Hegel's idealism and his evolutionary dialecticism flourished even as their religious foundation was being eroded.

After receiving a doctorate in philosophy at the University of Jena, Marx began to fuse his idealism with the radical materialism of the philosopher Ludwig Feuerbach. Like Spencer in London, Marx became a review journal editor in 1842. His articles and themes became so popular that his journal, *Rheinische Zeitung,* swiftly became one of the most popular in Prussia, and remained so until government authorities shut it down.

Marx and his new bride, whose father was a follower of the French Socialist Saint-Simon, moved to Paris to study French Communism. Calling in 1844 for "an uprising of the proletariat," Marx was expelled from France, went into exile in Brussels, and renounced his Prussian citizenship. After intensely turbulent years from 1845 to 1848—years in which, with his communist compatriot and co-author Friedrich Engels, he had helped to form the Communist League, write the historic *Communist Manifesto*, and organize groups to armed revolt—Marx became the very model of the modern practicing sociologist.

He was banished a second time from Paris in 1849 and settled with his wife and four small children in London. The years from 1850 to 1864 became ones of intellectual, social, and economic isolation. Two of the children died and his wife suffered from several emotional breakdowns. For half of these years the family subsisted in a two-room apartment in the poorest section of London, living on bread and potatoes.

Engels lent Marx what financial support he could and remained steadfastly loyal. In 1851, the *New York Tribune* hired Marx to be its European correspondent. Milk and soup could thus be put on the table once again, and over the next ten years Karl Marx contributed hundreds of articles and editorials to the paper. During the years of isolation and poverty, Marx continued disciplined historical, political, and economic studies on his own at the British Museum, until his rise as a correspondent. The culmination of this study was the publication of his masterpiece, *Das Kapital*, in 1867, as volume 1 of what became a three-volume work, with volumes 2 and 3 coming out posthumously under the editorship of Engels. It is this work that has earned Karl Marx his enduring and tremendously influential place in sociology. To activists everywhere in the world, however, Marx will always be remembered as the leading figure in the founding of the International Working Men's Association, which attracted nearly a million workers into what became the First International; and as a heroic figure in the revolutionary insurrection of the Paris Commune, which Engels termed history's first "dictatorship of the proletariat"—crushed by the French government in 1871.

Karl Marx did not think of himself as a sociologist. He did not read Comte until 1866 and rated the work negatively when he did. He paid no attention to Spencer, his contemporary; he never worked in the tradition of ethnology, he repudiated key aspects of organicism, and in his day he was defined as a political economist. None of this matters much, however, for the history of sociological practice. Marx's ideas have profoundly influenced the best sociologists of the twentieth century, and his actions in utilizing knowledge in the service of social progress, as he defined it, are legendary.

Unlike most social thinkers who went before him, Karl Marx believed deeply that understanding and interpreting the world—Hegel's mission—were incomplete. Instead, he held that thinkers about the human condition were obligated to transform human consciousness of the world and to help transform it in directions learned through their studies. The natural, material basis of human existence; capitalism and its relation to human labor; alienation; the dialectical, historical process through which class conflict generates its own destruction of the capitalist order; the place of false consciousness: these and other concepts form not a synthesistic system in the sense aspired to by Hegel, Comte, and Spencer, but a set of powerfully formative ideas set within a context of unremitting, close analysis of political and historical events. The ideas of no other social scientist have taken hold as widely in the common thinking of the world. Just as the ideas of John Locke and other philosophers of the Enlightenment shaped the American War of Independence, the Declaration of Independence, and the writing of the U.S. Constitution, so Karl Marx laid the intellectual foundations shared by revolutionaries, socialists, and many agents of social change in the years from 1848 to 1940.

Within that century, British socialism evolved along different lines; Marx was not a foundation for this evolution. Sociologists in Italy, France, and Germany paid close attention to and utilized his constructs, but sociologists in the United States paid his ideas little attention, if any, until the advent of the Great Depression in the 1930s.

Max Weber (1864–1920), educated in the law and political economy, extended the thought of Hegel and Marx into domains those two thinkers never visited. His sustained critique of economic materialism, first and most famously propounded in his book on *The Protestant Ethic and the Spirit of Capitalism*, extends through all his considerable body of work. However, he was also deeply interested in researching and theorizing about the nature of political authority, organizational bureaucracy, and crucial issues such as the place of value preferences in methodology. More importantly for practitioners, Max Weber was an active contributor to social policy, an influential advisor to political parties and government authorities, and a fierce opponent of German foreign and military policies in World War I. His scholarship has inspired generations of sociologists around the world and shapes research approaches in the field to this day.

Emile Durkheim (1858–1917) was the founder of the modern French school of sociology. His doctoral dissertation, *The Division of Labor in Society*, was prepared in the immediate aftermath of France's defeat in the Franco-Prussian War, the bloody conflicts with the Paris Commune that followed in 1871, and the collapse of the Second Empire (Durkheim 1933). French society and government were in extreme disarray and the question posed by Durkheim was simple but not easy: What is the cement that binds the social order? Most of his subsequent scholarship and sociological practice were dedicated to answering and applying new knowledge to this question. The modern conceptualization of anomie, social cohesion, social norms, and the formation and transmission of culture over time are the base of Durkheim's best thinking.

Durkheim's greatest contributions to sociology are theories and methods of empirical analysis. His second great treatise, *Suicide*, has remained for more than a century as a model of rigorous, comparative social analysis (Durkheim

1960). His sustained focus on categorizing and interpreting ethnological data from cultural anthropology has also become a hallmark of contemporary French social science in general.

What is important to the history of practice, however, is that Emile Durkheim was deeply invested in working on the social problems of his era. He taught for years at the high school level; worked on countless committees whose aims were to reform and update French pedagogy; studied under the founder of psychology in Germany, Wilhelm Wundt; and fashioned the first intellectual bridge between sociology and education, which he regarded as the practical extension of sociology and psychology.

Durkheim's scholarship and teaching also dealt in depth with applied criminology and penology. He played an important part in the campaign among the academics to exonerate Alfred Dreyfus, the French Jewish officer charged with spying on behalf of Germany (an infamous episode in the history of anti-Semitism in France). Durkheim always distinguished firmly between contributing to ideological positions and direct activism. He believed that a teacher or professor should not perform as an activist and should not guide the activism of his students.

Deemed a controversial figure and a Jew, Emile Durkheim, one of the greatest geniuses of France in his generation, was never elected to the Institute de France. It took him sixteen years after completing his doctorate to obtain a lectureship at the University of Bordeaux in social philosophy. Later, ten years after taking a professorship at the Sorbonne, Durkheim, still facing attacks from French nationalists who charged him with being German in his loyalties, lost his only son, who was killed while fighting for France in World War I. Durkheim died in 1917; whether of a broken heart, or of a stroke, or both, we cannot be sure.

CONVERGENT MOVEMENTS

We have focused quite singularly thus far upon the emergence of sociological ideas. Each of the thinkers presented here contributed to social policy and practice in his era, but each concentrated mightily upon the creation of theories, concepts, and methods of social inquiry. During the nineteenth century of European ferment, several movements took forms convergent with the rise of sociology, and those we mention here have become critical to sociological practice today.

Saint-Simon and Comte believed in the transformation of society under the rule of experts. They imagined socialism as a framework within which political disorder, class struggle, and the suffering of the poor would be mitigated by justice administered by a new kind of state. Francois Fourier had a different vision. In his socialist society, model communities would be ruled not by capitalist competition but by a shared search for the good life for all. He believed they would generate such civility and spontaneity that outside regulation by the state would become unnecessary. The Welshman Robert Owen created model villages, and imitations cropped up in several places in the new world of his times. Pierre-Joseph Proudhon surfaced as one of the founders of the anarchist tradition, in which greed, avarice, and exploitation were to be replaced by balances of equity and justice.

Later in the century, British Fabianism, grounded in non-Marxist ideas, took hold and grew swiftly in popularity. The Fabian Society founders (Beatrice Webb, Graham Wallas, Sidney Olivier, and George Bernard Shaw) pressed behind the scenes for social planning, social welfare legislation, and other reforms at the turn of the century. Fabians did not attempt to become a social movement; instead, they worked behind the scenes, in Shaw's words, "wire-pulling the government in order to get socialist measures passed." Gradualism was their strategy, and as influence through publications, the press, and education accumulated over decades, the Labor Party based its foundations on Fabianism.

The nineteenth century spawned not only sociology and socialism but also the confluent movement of social welfare. An exemplar was Charles Booth, the first person to survey systematically the *Labor and Life of the People in London* (1889–1891), who reported that a third of the city's people lived in poverty. The Charity Organization Society, a welfare agency for the destitute, was founded in London in 1869. Social insurance for retired workers began in Germany in 1883 and spread as a model across most of the Western countries during the next thirty years. The professionalization of social services followed, with schools; licensures; the formations of societies, councils, and agencies for maternal care, family planning, geriatric care, child welfare, adoption, and foster care services; and the creation of settlement houses and community centers.

Government-run social services other than social insurance did not come into being until the twentieth century. However, sociology's destiny was intertwined very closely, long before the governmental era, with the ideals of social cooperation, with sustained critiques against rampant capitalist exploitation of labor in the mines and factories, and with the agencies that evolved to offer help to the destitute and (in the United States) to immigrant families from abroad. The policy orientations of most nineteenth-century sociologists were, from the perspectives of that era in Europe, socialist in nature, and the commitment to organized social services made social work the eventual handmaiden of sociology.

THE BEGINNINGS OF SOCIOLOGICAL PRACTICE IN AMERICA

Lester F. Ward (1841–1913), an American, was born eleven years after Comte invented sociology. Ward was instrumental in establishing sociology as an academic discipline in the United States, yet he spent most of his life working as a civil servant in the federal government after earning degrees in botany and law. Ward did not become an academic until Brown University appointed him a professor of sociology in 1906, when he was sixty-five years of age.

Like Comte and Spencer before him, Ward was a positivist and an evolutionist schooled in the sciences. His sociology—brilliantly exposited in *Dynamic Sociology* (1883), *Pure Sociology* (1903), and *Applied Sociology* (1906)—treated the field as the prime foundation for all of the social sciences and as the vehicle for teaching the ways to achieve a better society. Ward's dynamics concern the fusion of social evolution with social engineering. His passion for the emergence of individualism lay in his belief that, through education and deliberate social planning, individuals of the future could optimize their intelligence and interpersonal competence.

Social scientists, Ward imagined, would some day assemble into a policy advisory committee in Washington, D.C., established to guide Congress toward acts conducive to the general welfare. He borrowed from Comte the term *sociocracy* to convey the import of his vision. Ward was a profound enthusiast for democracy, but in his era, well before the totalitarian regimes emerged in Europe, Ward believed innocently in the wisdom and rectitude of a generation of expert sociologists who would come to the fore in the 1890s and would function somewhat in the tradition of Plato's philosopher-kings who would come to rule the utopian Republic.

When the ideas of evolution, the British social science movement with its concern for political economy, and the philosophy of positivism came to

America, they were brilliantly unified in the writings of Lester Ward, but hundreds of other individuals in the years from 1870 to 1900 were thrilling to the beat of this seemingly new drummer, whose beat was essentially that of social reform. Socialism, even Fabianism, did not get included in the American march in those decades, and the work of Karl Marx did not gain an American following until much later. Still, there were reform impulses of all kinds that did make up the parade: the Social Gospel in Protestant seminaries and pulpits preached against the ravages of unbridled monopolism; Good Government groups sprang up in every city in search of ways to end the corruption and ineptitude of political machines and their bosses; and social welfare groups formed councils and agencies everywhere. Hundreds of Protestant ministers serving as part-time lecturers taught courses under such titles as political economy, social economics, general social science, and the like.

It was not until the sustained work of Lester Ward and of William Graham Sumner became widely read that sociology gradually gained American acceptance as a field in its own right. Not until colleges and universities undertook to invest in sociology could anyone make a living as a sociologist. Johns Hopkins University offered an array of courses in sociology as early as 1876, but did so through the department of history and politics.

It remained for the University of Chicago to establish the nation's first department of sociology, in 1892. Chicago itself was new, a kind of westward exportation of the Yale model. Sumner was at Yale and the founding leader of Chicago, William Rainey Harper, wanted to have everything Yale had and more. He funded the publication of the *American Journal of Sociology* in 1895, and within ten years enough sociologists had come out of Chicago and in from the Protestant pulpits to create the American Sociological Society.

Lester Ward was elected the Society's first president in 1905. His greatest book, *Applied Sociology*, was published in 1906. His presidential address and the book that followed made the reformative betterment of society the primary aim of sociology, or so he insisted. Ward emphasized that this great aim depended on the initial discovery and formulation of the principles that govern society.

Two trends sweeping across American higher education tended to divert this vision of Ward's. Colleges and universities themselves were becoming, in the words of economist Thorsten Veblen, commercialized as the beneficiaries and toadies of the giant corporations of the day. Chicago owed its entire creation to the Rockefellers of Standard Oil. Carnegie-Mellon University was the creation of the magnates after whom it was named. Established colleges were largely controlled by the religious denominations that funded them. With few exceptions, campuses were places of social and political conservatism at the close of the nineteenth century. Sociologists were admitted as a set of token liberals and reformers—in small numbers, and at the bottom of the totem pole of academic disciplines.

Secondly, the prevailing moral philosophies of the times were steeped in social Darwinism. The greatest publicist of this doctrine, William Graham Sumner, brought Spencerian sociology, the British focus on ethnology, and above all the ultra-American celebration of rugged individualism to the table of the nascent field of sociology. He taught at Yale University from 1872 to 1909 and mentored many future captains of industry and leading figures in the learned professions in the virtues of laissez-faire economics and government, individual liberty, and the innate inequalities among all humans.

Sumner posited a natural aristocracy of mental and physical abilities. Competition for resources and life chances, he taught, resulted in a beneficent elimination of the weak and the ill and enhanced the soundness and vigor of the upwardly mobile classes. He inveighed against the emergence of social welfare, celebrated the work ethic of the Protestant middle class, and convinced thousands of benighted learners of the misguided notion that good, meddlesome intentions toward helping the poor and the oppressed would contribute to undermining American life. Armed with formidable social scientific illustrations and case studies of these principles, Sumner's lectures, essays, and books became the foundation of conservative thought in his time.

Many American sociologists in the 1900–1920 era were thus creatures of their new academic appointments, which came ultimately from commercial and religious patrons. They were appointed selectively by administrators who were often earnest advocates of social Darwinism. Their reform, welfare, and real-world concerns for applying knowledge to better society came with them, but their new positions on campuses cut them off in many ways from opportunities to pursue reforms. Campuses, with some important exceptions, catered almost exclusively to white, male, middle-class students, and faculty were often isolated from the surrounding communities by large class and cultural gaps between town and gown.

THE CHICAGO SCHOOL AND ITS EFFECTS

John D. Rockefeller gave $15 million to what had been the Baptist-owned Chicago University to revive it and make it into the University of Chicago.

The new university was the first in North America to emphasize graduate studies and research. William Graham Sumner at Yale and Lester Ward at Brown spent their years lecturing to undergraduates, for example. William Rainey Harper, the founding president at Chicago, assembled a sizeable group of the most distinguished scholars of England, Germany, and the United States; made them department heads; put them in clusters within the Cambridge-style quadrangles of the new campus; and gave the formative task in sociology to Albion Woodbury Small, then president of Colby College in Maine.

The son of a distinguished Congregational clergyman, Small himself had graduated from Newton Theological Seminary in Massachusetts before embarking on years of graduate study in history, economics, and political science at universities in Germany. Small quickly surfaced as the best leader in the ranks of the newly assembled economists, anthropologists, political scientists, and sociologists, and in 1905 Harper appointed him Dean of the Graduate School of Arts and Literature, which then contained the social sciences.

Albion Small was a talented organizer as well as a dedicated academic scholar. He recruited such great sociologists of the day as Charles Henderson, George Vincent, and William I. Thomas onto the faculty, and he joined with Lester Ward and Franklin Giddings of Columbia in organizing the American Sociological Society and in mounting intellectual protests against the competitive individualism and aggressive social Darwinism of the times. He had little involvement in the real-world application of sociology, however. Late in his career he wrote about how the social sciences could guide government by helping to design more rational social policy, but most of his work formed a sort of conventional bridge between moral philosophy and the new social sciences. Unlike Lester Ward, he was neither positivistic nor applied in his approaches.

The University of Chicago got off to a very fast and memorable start in the history of sociology in America, thanks to the leadership of Albion Small. A school of collaborative inquiry, teaching, and real-world practice grew up around Robert Park, who joined W. I. Thomas in the young, new department in 1913. Their shared intellectual concerns were with the study of European immigrants, as in *The Polish Peasant in Europe and America* (Thomas and Znaniecki 1918–1920); and with the social mapping of Chicago, which they treated as a laboratory city for sociological inquiry. Park was both a journalist and a sociologist. He had investigated Belgian atrocities in the Belgian Congo, been a ghost writer for Booker T. Washington, and written press releases for a living, as well as having studied sociology as a graduate student in Germany.

Under the broad label *urban studies*, the focus for Thomas, Park, and Ernest Burgess became ethnicity and race. Ernest Burgess joined the department in 1918 as the mainstay of empirical research. Faculty and students were housed close to one another in a tower of Harper Library. Ten years later they were housed in what came to be called "1126," the street number of the Social Sciences building, where the social intimacy and constant mutual exploration of social issues continued.

Robert Park had been the director of the Chicago Urban League. As he and Thomas pioneered in race-relations and ethnic studies, Burgess laid out the framework of his concentric-circle ecology of cities, modeled very directly on Chicago. Graduate student research worked freely on questions that rose out of the combination of these specialties.

One of the first African American students to join the Chicago School was Charles S. Johnson (Robbins 1997). He arrived fresh from Virginia with two dollars in his pocket in 1917. After serving in France in the Great War, Johnson returned to Chicago in 1919 in time to suffer through the worst race riot in that city's history, in which twenty-three blacks and eighteen whites died. White mobs initiated and maintained the riot but blacks fought back. City fathers created a commission to study the riot, and Johnson became that commission's associate executive director. The result was *The Negro in Chicago* (1922), all of which was planned by Charles Johnson and half of which was written by him. It is a landmark in the annals of applied sociology. A few years later, Johnson became director of the National Urban League and settled into Harlem, where he became part of the Harlem Renaissance. It is important for the history of sociological practice to note that Chicago did not award Charles Johnson a Ph.D., although he was addressed as "Dr. Johnson" for the remainder of his life. We do not know why this was, but we speculate that a combination of racial prejudice and highly applied research may have played a part. In those days the requirements for a Ph.D. were much looser than they are today, and a published monograph of the quality and magnitude of *The Negro in Chicago* would have resulted in a Ph.D. under most circumstances. In any event, Johnson went on to a very distinguished career as president of Fisk University, where he brought Robert Park to the faculty in 1937. Another distinguished applied sociologist who was African American, Franklin Frazier, came a decade after Johnson to study in the Chicago School.

Many other sociologists contributed to the Chicago School, which began its decline with the retirement of Robert Park but cast an attractive shadow that extended across the social sciences long after the school itself declined.

The roster includes William F. Ogburn, Herbert Blumer, George Herbert Mead, Samuel Stouffer, Everett Hughes, Paul Lazersfeld, Leonard Cottrell, Nelson Foote, Otis Dudley Duncan, David Riesman, Phillip Hauser, and many others. By World War II, however, the Chicago School's prestige and dominance had begun to slip. Several Big Ten universities, particularly the University of Wisconsin at Madison, had come up fast, and Columbia and Harvard had begun to dominate in the East.

The aspect of the Chicago School of greatest importance to sociological practice, we are confident, was its implicit commitment to building both pure and applied sociology. The articles in *The American Journal of Sociology*, books published by faculty and graduate students, and the papers presented each year at the School's Society for Social Research were as often devoted to applications as to social theory and research methodology. Practical work and work undertaken to improve society were received with genuine interest. Ernest Burgess's own longitudinal study of engaged couples, begun in 1938 and continued until 1960, was devoted to his conviction that good research would enable couples and their counselors to predict the likelihood of marital compatibility and stability. Foote and Cottrell (1958) and colleagues worked on methods with which to train and induce increased interpersonal competence. The idea that doing good sociology entailed fusing the practical with the pure was a norm within the Chicago School. It did not break apart until after World War II.

HULL HOUSE

The Chicago School admitted women as students, and it had a female professor soon after its founding. For the most part, however, the female graduate students were not sent out to take up faculty posts on the dozens of campuses that were building sociology departments between 1900 and 1920. One of the solutions, hit upon first by Fabians in England, was to create "settlement houses" where highly educated women could volunteer time to work with women of the working and lower classes. Toynbee Hall was founded in 1884 in East London and Hull House opened in Chicago in 1889 (Fish 1985). The aim, in the case of Hull House, was to restore communication between the college educated and the working poor and to help improve conditions of life in the cities.

Chicago's population doubled between 1880 and 1890 and doubled again between 1890 and 1900. As it swelled to host Irish, Polish, and Italian immigrants, it swelled again to receive hundreds of thousands of African Americans from the Deep South. Its political corruption, business savagery, and labor exploitation, along with its physical filth and overcrowding, attracted more than its share of reformers. Women joined Jane Addams at her Hull House to advocate for housing, health care, child care, and education for the families of the newly arriving poor. In the circles of urban good government, welfare reformers, social workers, and urban planners of the times, Chicago was the dynamic place to be.

Albion Small in fact offered Jane Addams a half-time appointment in 1913, twenty-four years after she arrived to create Hull House. She apparently did not accept that offer, but she did teach intermittently in the Extension Division of the university and had other connections with the faculty and graduate students. Hull House was, from their point of view, a wonderful urban laboratory for applied research.

One of the enthusiasts was W. I. Thomas, whose first wife, Helen Thomas, was deeply involved in work on the suffrage and peace movements at Hull House. Professor Thomas used to dine there frequently. Hull House volunteers established the Juvenile Court and the Juvenile Protection Association of Chicago, both of which maintained applied social research connections with the university into the 1950s. George Herbert Mead became the founding vice president of the Immigrants Protective League, created at Hull House and hosted there as early as 1908. Mead also took part in labor strikes in the early 1900s, including the strikes of Chicago garment workers, and he was a champion of women's suffrage. Of great importance to the role of Hull House and its women leaders is that this was the setting and these were the sociologists who accomplished the most in American efforts to go beyond soapbox advocacy and muckraking and to link reform planning with careful surveys of the needs of the urban poor, following in the tradition of Charles Booth in London. Hull House lives on to this day. Without the genius of its first quarter-century, it is questionable whether sociological practice would have emerged at all in America.

The combined influence of the Chicago School and Hull House was great enough to shape careers and student learning in regions of the United States distant from the Midwest. An example of this was Wellesley College in Massachusetts. As Mary Jo Deegan noted in her history of "Sociology at Wellesley College: 1900–1919" (1985), women were barred from nearly all of the nation's universities. Even if all universities had been open to them, very few would have enrolled, because high schools with college preparatory courses available to women did not open until the 1850s. When Wellesley first opened its doors in 1875, it had only one female faculty member who had taught at a college before.

A department of sociology evolved gradually at Wellesley out of courses offered in the Department of History and Economics. As their popularity grew, courses named "Socialism," "Statistical Study of Certain Economic Problems," "Social Economics," "Labor Problems," and "General Sociology," were offered.

Sociologists at Wellesley were associated closely with the University of Chicago and with the laboratory of social service and inquiry created there by Jane Addams. Marion Talbot of Wellesley was the first woman recruited to join the Chicago Department of Sociology when it opened its doors in 1892. Talbot's protégé Edith Abbott took a Ph.D. from Chicago and returned to Wellesley, where she worked with others to build sociology into the offerings of the other elite women's colleges of the East. Talbot, Abbott, and other Wellesley sociologists worked closely with and intermittently at Hull House from 1908 to 1920.

Women sociologists of the day were deeply involved in the formation and elaboration of social work. They were steeped in Webb's Fabian socialism, and some were world-class leaders of the pacificist movement. Two of them, Emily Greene Balch and Jane Addams, became, in the words of Congressmen leading the Red Scare Search of 1919, "the most dangerous women in America . . . bolsheviks . . . conspirators linked in a spider web to overthrow the government" (Deegan 1985, 105). As late as 1926, when the Red Scare had faded, Senator Thomas Bayard spoke to the United States Senate in these terms:

It is of the utmost significance that practically all the radicalism started among women in the United States centers about Hull House, Chicago, and the Children's Bureau at Washington, with a dynasty of Hull House graduates in charge of it since its creation.

It has been shown that both the legislative program and the economic program—"social welfare" legislation and "bread and peace" propaganda for internationalization of the food, farms, and raw materials of the world—find their chief expression in persons, organizations, and bureaus connected with Hull House. (Cited in Deegan 1985, 105–6)

The trustees of Wellesley College decided to discontinue Balch's faculty appointment in the spring of 1917, because of her pacifist opposition to involvement in World War I. Her academic career was thus cut off when she was fifty-two years old. She published many books and more than a hundred articles on the sociology of women, labor, and social agencies, and her work for the League of Nations and later for the planning of the United Nations had substantial influence among international relations experts. Jane Addams won the Nobel Peace Prize in 1931, and Emily Balch won it in 1946 for her leadership of the Women's International Organization for Peace and Freedom. No other American woman won this great award until it was granted to Jody Williams in 1997 for her leadership of the movement to ban land mines.

Wellesley College's contributions to sociology have—with the exception noted by Deegan of Rose Laub Coser, who taught there for a few years in the 1950s—been negligible. The firing of Emily Balch marked the beginning of its descent into mediocrity. Connections to social work disappeared gradually and women's studies were submerged, along with the early prominence of sociology itself, until the 1970s.

THE GREAT DEPRESSION AND WORLD WAR II

The student of sociological practice should keep in mind how small the profession was in 1930. The American Sociological Society had fewer than 800 members in that year. Perhaps 200 of them affiliated out of interest, but in fact were educated in theology, social work, and other related, friendly fields. The Society was not an organization designed to serve professionals. It was open to a wide range of participants, a condition that prevailed until the close of the 1950s. The field was growing on the eve of the Great Depression in 1929, but the growth sprang from the rise of undergraduate course offerings. The typical college in 1930 posted about twelve three-credit courses in sociology—enough to constitute a major concentration—with six of the courses being sufficient for a minor concentration. By 1940, most liberal arts students in America had taken at least one introductory sociology course. These students did not aspire to enter the field of sociology, however; they hoped to become high school social studies teachers, social workers, personnel and labor relations staff, or government employees.

Despite the orientation of these undergraduates, though, the increasingly dominant graduate research centers of the times included very few practice-centered professors. In his 1929 presidential address to the American Sociological Society, William F. Ogburn of the Chicago School declared, "Sociology as a science is not interested in making the world a better place to live.

. . . Science is interested in one thing only, to wit, discovering new knowledge" (Pettigrew 1980, xxii). It would appear from his grammar that Ogburn had the hubris to believe he knew what sociology was (or perhaps ought to be) "interested in," and he even knew what the god Science was solely interested in. Science for Ogburn was an overarching whole. Paradoxically, Ogburn was at that same moment completing a panel report for President Herbert Hoover on *Recent Social Trends* as he made this pronouncement. The report relied heavily upon utterly practical data from the Census Bureau and from the work then emanating from survey researchers.

The New Deal response to the Great Depression drew many sociologists into government service. They joined the original staffs of the Social Security Administration, the Public Works Administration, criminal justice and corrections, the Bureau of Labor Statistics, the Women's Bureau, the Children's Bureau, and the administrative units of the relief and work programs in the states and regions. College- and university-based sociologists were drawn into efforts to research, plan, and implement relief, welfare, and development programs. Ernest Burgess, for example, managed the work of some thirty WPA statistical clerks as part of social, economic, and demographic mapping of Chicago and Cook County. Rural sociologists were at work on community organization in the U.S. Department of Agriculture and in the Agricultural Experiment Stations.

Academic elitists were embracing scientism just as the practitioners were being mobilized to assist a collapsing Western world engulfed by joblessness, despair, vast and deep unrest, and famine. Race relations and the civil rights movement during the 1930s also offer a case in point. Donald S. Young's book, *American Minority Peoples,* published in 1932, was the first major textbook offered in the teaching of race relations. W. E. B. DuBois, the most prominent figure in civil rights at the time, was ignored by the white sociological establishment, even though his movement was achieving legal victories. Black sociologists, with but a small handful of exceptions, taught in black colleges. The profession was as segregated as the society at large.

Gunnar Myrdal's project, begun in 1939, and culminating in 1944 with the publication of *An American Dilemma*, was widely regarded as a sociological enterprise (Clayton 1995). Charles S. Johnson, Arthur Paper, T. J. Woofter, and others from the ranks of black sociologists participated heavily. Arnold Rose was co-author of the final draft, and Samuel Stouffer took over the management of the research effort when Myrdal was forced by the war to return to Sweden. This was applied sociology at its finest.

World War II stimulated the development of sociological practice. The mobilization of all human as well as industrial resources drew significantly upon all social scientists. They entered the armed services, espionage and military intelligence, the Office of War Information, and many other units of government and industry as these were fashioned into weapons of war. Samuel Stouffer gathered a very talented and sizeable staff to create the survey research branch of the Army, producing the two-volume classic, *The American Soldier: Adjustment During Army Life,* and *The American Soldier: Combat and its Aftermath* (1949). The Air Force used social psychologists as part of the design of training for paratroopers, and the Navy used them to work on problems associated with the selection and training of crews for submarines. These are just a small set of examples of the many applications that came out of practice during wartime.

Paul Lazersfeld and many others pioneered during the 1940s in marketing and consumer research (Lazersfeld, Berelson, and Gaudet 1948). The application of survey technology to audience research made the mass media, from films to radio, increasingly creatures of ratings and pilot testing. Opinion polling itself was evolving rapidly during the same period, as national elections, campaign materials, and policy debates were brought under the grand survey umbrella between 1936 and 1948. Columbia created its Bureau of Applied Social Research, Chicago its National Opinion Research Center. There was also the Survey Research Center at Michigan, the Laboratory of Social Relations at Harvard, the Institute of Human Relations at Yale, the Public Opinion Laboratory at the University of Washington, and a handful of others, which together made up a national network of applied sociology in those years.

Sociological faculty thus got deeply involved in applied projects during the 1940s, but they kept these projects carefully separate from their "pure" scholarship and teaching for their universities. Graduate students served as a kind of human bridge between the academic side and the staffing of the projects.

THE HEYDAY OF AMERICAN SOCIOLOGY

American sociology, and practice along with it, burst its old seams after World War II. There were fewer than a thousand members of ASS in 1940, but there were more than four thousand in 1954. An estimated 2 percent of undergraduates majored in sociology after the war, but the number of students enrolled in college more than doubled as a result of the G.I. Bill and a rising tide of women students; thus, the number of would-be sociologists more than doubled. Sixty institutions offered graduate studies and in 1953, 141 Ph.D. degrees in sociology were awarded. As Hans Zetterberg noted at that time,

Most sociological projects undertaken in the United States are headed by a university professor. Most of these projects involve a staff of several people in addition to the person in charge. There exists in these departments a tradition of research practice, short-cuts in securing and processing research data which authors who write texts on principles of research normally fail to mention . . . but which constitute an informal laboratory tradition without which research would be a great deal more cumbersome. This uncodified body of research techniques must be learned . . . in association with those who already possess it. The excellency of American training in sociology is in no small part due to the widespread possibility for students to participate as research assistants in projects where they can learn this uncodified research tradition. What to them might appear as primarily a way to finance their graduate studies actually becomes an essential part of their sociological training. (Zetterberg 1956, 11)

The cost of the typical sociological project in the early 1950s averaged about $3,500. A local area survey might cost no more than $3,000 to $10,000, whereas a national probability sample could be collected and analyzed for about $125,000. Graduate students could be retained as assistants for a few hundred dollars a term and could be obligated to give as much sweat equity in overtime as the project demanded.

This arrangement is of immense historical significance for sociology because the sociological practice that took place off campus, in nonacademic settings, grew tremendously in scale as this arrangement failed to meet the demands of the 1960s. Corporate, governmental, and military demands for social scientific research and development grew so huge after 1957 that the old apprentice system could not accommodate the demand. The Department of Defense, marketing and organizational development arms of industry, the Agency for International Development, UNESCO, and the War on Poverty waged by the U.S. Office of Economic Opportunity did not want the older-style, three-year, three-person grant project. Their needs were large and immediate. The work often entailed program planning, demonstration and pilot human service projects, and program evaluations. Many of these tasks were exceptionally difficult to translate into academic publications; many were socially risky and controversial; and most took full-time efforts. Contracts came to replace grants as clients became increasingly specific about the pieces of work they wanted completed.

Approximately 100 social science research and development firms were established between 1960 and 1975. They spanned the United States, from the Stanford Research Institute in California to Abt Associates in Massachusetts. About one-third were concentrated in Maryland and Virginia in the suburbs surrounding Washington, D.C., where firms whose staff did work for federal agencies became known to journalists as "Beltway Bandits." In the 1980s, in response to requirements for monitoring and evaluation imposed on developing countries by the World Bank and the International Monetary Fund, one or more counterpart firms were established in every nation. Military service branches, industries, and businesses began, in the same era, to draw on the same or parallel research and development (R&D) firms to conduct their inquiries and to do their planning.

For the first time since 1900, then, sociologists in large numbers could aspire to careers outside of college and university departments of sociology. The transition period (that is, the years from 1955 to 1970) constitute what we call the heyday of American sociology. There were an abundant number of positions open within the academy and on its fringes, permitting rapid employment, career options, and new sources of research revenue and individual income. Clever senior sociologists learned to move smoothly between their lifetime tenured professorships, and similar appointments, to management and project director roles in the emerging consulting firms. Some in fact created firms for themselves while continuing some of their teaching and mentoring activities with graduate student apprentices. Others created highly applied institutes and centers within their universities and purchased release time from their regular academic obligations in order to carry on the new contract work. Still others took turns rotating between their professorships and temporary government positions, from which they dispensed project patronage to their colleagues and former apprentices. It was an extraordinarily abundant and profitable period for sociologists, psychologists, social statisticians, and above all, economists. Each year, moreover, additional hundreds of young social scientists who undertook one or another nonacademic project in one of these firms did not return to the academy to build a professorial career.

Subfields of sociology were growing in this period as well. Marriage and family behavior were fueling the emergence of marriage counseling as a licensed clinical specialty. Criminology became increasingly buttressed by the rise of the criminal justice administration and police science professions. Behavioral organization surfaced as a major feature in programs of business management. Mental health and illness studies grew rapidly and came to involve sociologists deeply in a movement toward deinstitutionalization of mental patients on the one hand and clinical interventions in alternative treatments on the other. Studies of small group behavior and related social psychological studies into consumer preferences, mass communications, and processes of social conflict, attitude change, and social influence grew very rapidly in this era. The sociology of education took off as well, with substantial investments from the U.S. Office of Education and with the addition of research and demonstration centers to schools of education. With these changes, the professionalization of the subfields of sociology itself began. Thus, applied work left the cores of the academic departments of sociology and alighted in the professional schools and colleges. The historic departments became service-course carriers for undergraduates traveling over from those schools, although they maintained a small stream of doctoral candidates in the academic field.

THE COMING CRISIS

Sociological theorist Alvin Gouldner published *The Coming Crisis in Western Sociology* in 1970. It embodied, expressed, and reflected the extreme cultural turmoil of its times. From Paris to London to New York to Berkeley, the Baby Boomers, those millions of children born immediately after World War II, had begun to come of age. Their great numbers, the increasing social power of youth, the economies of the times, and the critical gulf between their value preferences and the surviving mores from the pre-war West, impelled a culture shift of the first magnitude. The functionalism, grand theoreticalism, and positivistic value neutrality of conventional, academic sociology was dead, said Gouldner, and a socially relevant sociology was being born.

Student activism became the vehicle of cultural change, and sociology students were in the vanguard. As journalist Abe Peck noted:

The number of U.S. students would double between 1960 and 1966, and some would seek Left-oriented change. In 1960, students from the Berkeley campus protested capital punishment at San Quentin, and were hosed at House Un-American Activities Committee hearings in San Francisco. In 1961, they began going South for civil rights; in 1963, they were among more than seven hundred arrested during an anti-racist-hiring protest at a San Francisco hotel. By fall, 1964, Berkeley had its veteran demonstrators.

The nearly four-month Free Speech struggle began [with University of California students on the Berkeley Campus] over whether or not students could raise money for causes on campus. . . .

Events quickened when students surrounded a squad car containing an arrested dropout-activist named Jack Weinberg, who'd been soliciting funds for CORE [Congress of Racial Equality]. Weinberg later would provide a slogan for the times: "Don't trust anybody over thirty!" (Peck 1985, 17–18)

Revolutionary fervor spread in waves across the United States. Fueled by the civil rights movement initially, activists added Vietnam War resistance and then other causes to their movement. As campus unrest reached as far downward as junior high schools between 1967 and 1970, Columbia University and University of Chicago graduate students came into the forefront of the movement. Many of them were in sociology. Todd Gitlin, a Harvard B.A. in 1963, became a journalist, a voice for key parts of the movement, and, ultimately, a professor of sociology at Berkeley more than a decade later. His career was indicative of the countercultural trends that engulfed much of Western sociology at the close of the 1960s.

The academic sociology establishment, composed very predominantly of white males educated between 1940 and 1960, came under attack by the social activists, as did almost every other part of the higher educational system. The American Sociological Association itself came under substantial attack from the radical caucuses on the Left. Membership splintered for a time along ideological lines, and some of the subgroups formed at this time live on as sections and associations to this day.

As Paul Baker and William Rau observed in their report on recent trends in the field, however,

In the . . . 1960s, sociologists were optimistic about building a stronger academic discipline and their optimism was fueled by an enormous expansion in undergraduate enrollments. . . . Undergraduate enrollments grew not because of left politics but because of the rapid expansion of the social service sector. Mushrooming numbers occurred prior to establishment of undergraduate programs in social services, especially bachelors programs in social work and criminal justice. During the 1960s, sociology was still the logical choice for many students who liked people or wanted to work with the dispossessed. Much to the students' surprise, they would learn in literature, such Berger's *Invitation to Sociology*, that sociologists have little interest in working with people. The 1960s can be described as the decade in which sociology continued to advance its cultural purity and unwittingly became further alienated from its undergraduate constituency. (Baker and Rau 1990, 172)

The countercultural era, in its brevxity, did not resolve the issue of the relation between sociology and social activism. Within its larger context, however, many sociologists in the years from 1964 to 1974 became more deeply involved in direct work with the needs of the poor, racial and ethnic minorities, and groups (such as migrant workers) suffering economic oppression than in any previous period of sociology in the United States. A change in the cultural ethos combined with changes in opportunities to work with grassroots organizations and with neighborhood leaders, union leaders, and civil rights leaders. Women were beginning to play a much more influential role in the social sciences and the revision of evidence about gender differences was building quickly, as were the ties between the new feminism and the new sociology.

BEYOND THE CRISIS

All of these changes, when combined with the rising number of sociologists entering nonacademic positions and applied centers on campuses, gave sociological practice and applied uses for the discipline an appeal that had been lacking for decades. Louis Wirth had written an article on clinical sociology that was published in Chicago's *American Journal of Sociology* in 1931. He called for "[a] rationale for clinical practice that recognizes the value of theory and the opportunity to combine theory and practice for benefit of both" (cited in Glass and Fritz 1982, 3). Wirth, a psychologist with affiliations in sociology, defined *clinical* in terms of modern medicine, where the emphasis is on the case method and on diagnosis, study, and treatment of whole individuals rather than subsets of pathologies. *Clinical sociology*, he wrote, "is a clinical label for those insights, methods of approach, and techniques which the science of sociology can contribute to the understanding and of persons whose behavior or personality problems bring them under the care of clinics for study and treatment" (Wirth 1931; cited in Glass and Fritz 1982, 8).

Wirth's vision was generally ignored until the beginning of the 1970s, when the sociology of medicine began to mature into inclusion within medical, nursing, and allied health schools and then to become a part of hospital and university units in behavioral medicine. Simultaneously, it was in this period that sociologists began to practice clinically within mental health and family social agencies. In 1976, sociologists banded together to establish what became the Sociological Practice Association (SPA), first named the Clinical Sociology Association. The Wirthian conception of clinical practice was in turn refined and expanded to include intervention activities and services of many kinds, including labor unions, communities, government agencies, and corporations.

The Society for Applied Sociology (SAS) was formed in 1978. It was pioneered by Alex Boros, who, with other colleagues in the Midwest, was distressed by the absence of applied concerns and applied work in the papers and conferences of the North Central Sociological Association. The driving factors were the same as those impelling the formation of the SPA: a rising number of nonacademic sociologists, a rising number of academics who engaged part-time in applied and clinical practice, and a change in the ethos of all the social sciences in the aftermath of the 1960s. These combined with one other vital event to change the status of sociological practice.

That event was the decline, beginning in about 1974 and continuing to this day, in employment opportunities for sociologists on faculties as tenure-track instructors. Numbers of sociology majors among undergraduates declined on many campuses, while rising numbers of M.A. and Ph.D. candidates were coming out and qualifying for professional employment. As students voted with their feet to move into schools of business and other highly applied concentrations, both humanities and social science courses went begging for undergraduate takers even as they generated larger numbers of advanced graduate students. Academic professors of sociology, and the American Sociological Association which they controlled, fretted the question but did not know what to do about it. They had what Robert K. Merton would have termed a trained incapacity to expand the occupational frontiers of the very field they had worked so hard to make both positivistic and academically respectable as a science.

As the number of unemployed and very underemployed sociologists rose during the 1980s, the leadership of the ASA continued to be unable or unwilling to deal effectively with nonacademic career development options. As the great graduate centers cut back on the numbers of doctoral students they enrolled in that period, practitioners took their futures into their own hands.

They strengthened their new organizations. SPA began to produce a journal, *Clinical Sociology*. Later, the SAS began to produce its *Journal of Applied*

Sociology. The ASA established a section on Sociological Practice and it agreed
to create and fund a journal, *The Sociological Review*. That agreement was
reached by the ASA Executive Council in 1986, but squabbles and divisions
led to a delay, and the journal did not materialize until 1990. I had agreed to
be its founding editor and I joined the editorial committee of the ASA in
1989, ostensibly as an equal among peers. It quickly became obvious that the
"pure academics" in the committee and on the council were politely hostile.
The journal came under fire almost immediately from academic purists and
was summarily discontinued as an unwarranted expense in 1992. Alex Boros,
Jan Fritz, Howard Freeman, Peter Rossi, and William Foote Whyte were among
those who supported and assisted the fledgling journal, but their efforts came
to naught when the executive council of the ASA voted to terminate it.

In the same period (1975–1990), many departmental faculties looked for
ways in which to adapt. Their undergraduate enrollments were shrinking and
their graduate students were facing unemployment unless they invented new
ways to survive. Use of one way that had become popular in the 1960s intensified in this period: academic sociologists expanded the range and volume of
their service courses for professional schools, and many younger faculty found
niches in the faculties of those schools. This was particularly true for the fields
of health care, criminal justice, and business management.

Other faculties began to fashion degree programs, especially at the M.A.
level, in applied sociology and, increasingly, under the more inclusive banner
of sociological practice. By 1995, there were more than 100 such degree programs. There were also some doctoral and undergraduate concentrations being offered under these names. Workshops and internships in human service,
state agency, and business settings were built into these programs of study,
and these expanded rapidly into the gerontology, juvenile justice, corrections,
and public safety fields. Courses in policy analysis and program evaluation
sprang into being. Training in data collection and computer-based data analysis
came to the forefront, and field research and qualitative case studies took on
a new respectability.

INTERPRETIVE CONCLUSION

Every physical and life science has as its twin sister a field of engineering.
Applied physics, electrical engineering, biotechnology, computer applications,
and clinical medicine are unmistakable examples worldwide. The largest and
most expansively dynamic social science, psychology, with its thirty-three pro-

fessional divisions, has its clinical psychology and counseling psychology twins, along with other applied fields. Political science has its counterparts in public administration and public policy or public affairs specialists. Economics has its schools of management, with applied fields in accounting and marketing, among others.

Sociology began as an intellectual orphan and continues as such to this day. As one of the original and major departures from the hegemony of theology and moral philosophy, it became a magnificent orphan of the Age of Reason, because it was rejected by all who believed that its mission belonged to religion and to the mores and customs of civilization. From its beginnings in the books of Condorcet, Saint-Simon, and Comte, though, its grand aim was to become a science whose knowledge about society would prove to be prescriptive for progressive improvement of the human condition.

Its applied features did not take root anywhere other than in the discourse of European intellectuals and the political movements of communists and Fabian socialists during much of its first century of life. Sociology contributed powerfully to the raising of public consciousness about the nature of society and the polity during the second half of the nineteenth century. Reform movements and movements to create a general social science aimed at reform sprang up everywhere. Lester Ward's volumes of theory and interpretation referred in every chapter to the ways in which social progress could be shaped, clarified, and induced through the use of sociological ideas and facts. At the same time, the social evolutionists, Herbert Spencer and William Graham Sumner, were preaching that human groups should not interfere with the natural equilibrium of societies.

In the early twentieth century, at least by 1925, sociology went academic. The orphan was adopted by colleges and universities throughout the Western world. Sociology took to this adoption with a satisfaction akin to what it would be like to find heaven on earth; its adherents permitted women and students of color to study with them but not to live at home after graduation. When sociologists tried to make more of it, or when they behaved like unruly ingrates (as did Emily Balch), the academy cast them out into settlement houses and government bureaus.

I have noted that the impulse to intervene—to help, to work closely with oppressed and needy groups in society—never diminished. These impulses impelled the creation of sociology in the first place. They were carried in on endless waves of freshmen and sophomores from 1890 to 1990. The same impulses detracted from the academic cultural purity of the discipline, however, and were resisted with vigor by the leading figures in the field after 1930. Those who worked to build a pure science of society also wanted to attract external and institutional prestige and support for their mission. Their vision of practice was as morally inspired as was the vision of the practitioners: a great and powerful science, drawing into its midst the best and brightest minds of the times, and capable of social prediction and analysis of a valid and reliable kind. Students who wanted to "work with people," or to "help people," along with faculty who emphasized human service and social activism, were the perceived enemies of this lofty aspiration. These tendencies were also generic in degree programs in theological schools, education, and nursing, to name just a few of the helping professions, and academic sociologists were strongly disposed to fix firm boundaries between their discipline and the professions, which they regarded as suffused with moral biases and an incomplete foundation in social structure.

Sociological practice as such thus made very little headway between 1880 and 1980. The context in which sociological engineering would take root was missing, as was a clear conception of how practitioners should go about efforts at human, group, and organizational betterment. The context and the methodologies of application in the years since 1980 grew up outside of academic departments in the applied research, development, and human service firms and agencies that took root in the 1960s. They were symbiotic, drawing on the part-time involvement of the academics, but they were also nonacademically designed and sponsored. Nevertheless, new academic departments followed apace as these new settings became ones from which to recruit and then in which to place students.

The domain of practice remains muddled to this day. The political pendulum in England and then in the United States swung, from 1980 to 2000, from liberal to conservative policies, just as the vision of sociology as an applied field was gaining new footholds. I witnessed bumper stickers at the time of Ronald Reagan's election, for example, which read "Help Stamp Out Social Science." With the work of the Sociological Practice Association, the Society for Applied Sociology, the Sociological Practice Section of the American Sociological Association, and the advent of other organizations such as the American Evaluation Association and the Academy of Criminal Justice, an aura of conceptual refinement and clarity evolved around practice, but all these groups had to cope with disheartening trends in the larger society.

Real growth in quality has taken place, yet the muddle that began with

Comte about the place of social action in sociology persists. The organizations named here have yet to unify around missions, standards, or activities, for example; fifteen years after graduate studies in applied sociology were inaugurated, this book represents the first general textbook to be published on the subject.

The muddle is less exasperating than it once was. Sociologists with M.A.s and Ph.D.s who enter careers outside the academy often lose their identification with sociology in the process. They join teams where disciplinary attachments are of little or no value because the teams are composed of men and women from many different fields, who are presumed to be capable of working together on a client's question or need. Yet, there is a possibility that, in the coming century, those who commit to practice will be welcomed wholeheartedly into the associations controlled by the discipline, and will be able to contribute to ᵗhe transformation of those associations through their experience and knowledge.

Although it remains muddled, sociological practice has also achieved considerable conceptual refinement in recent years. The early positivists regarded practice as a matter of strategic social criticism. They sought to equip a class (in their case scientists and other intellectuals) with knowledge that would make rationally defensible their own ascendant power (Gitlin 1995, 214). Marx and Engels and, in a different way, the Fabian socialists sought to align their social criticism with fledgling labor movements or with power elites and to harness social policy ideas to engines of change.

After World War II, as sociology recast itself increasingly as a profession and as a value-detached empirical science, this function of practice diminished greatly. Sociological ideas were used by thousands of social critics and commentators, but sociologists did not host radio or television talk shows or write many popular social commentaries. When they spoke, it was most often as professional experts retained to testify or to marshal and sift narrow sets of evidence. When they went beyond this, they lacked both support from the academic club and much of an audience at large.

Practice has become, since the 1950s, a kind of service technology for foundations, government agencies, and corporate industries. This is the technology of focus groups, questionnaires, opinion surveys, population analyses, and program evaluations. In substance, the technology is harnessed to a variety of other professional domains—in health care, law, environmental policy implementation, and corrections, for example. Sociologists in practice are thus frequently at the beck and call of decision makers and policy implementors in other fields and, as technicians, they do not often aspire or presume to social criticism.

Practice has also become a matter of participation in direct human services and service systems: drug and alcohol treatment, housing for the homeless, behavioral medicine, and sociotherapy within mental health clinics, to give just a few examples. It has become, in the tradition of Emily Balch and Jane Addams, the practice of social advocacy of change from within institutions of service. Finally, sociological practice has been a profession in which positive change itself is invented and demonstrated experimentally or through participative programs.

REFERENCES

Baker, P. J., and W. C. Rau. 1990. The cultural contradictions of teaching sociology. In *Sociology in America*, edited by H. Gans, 169–87. Newbury Park, Calif.: Sage Publications.

Bernard, L. L., and J. Bernard. 1943. *Origins of American Sociology: The Social Science Movement in the United States.* New York: Thomas Y. Crowell. Reissue, New York: Russell and Russell, 1965.

Booth, C. 1889–1891. *Labour and Life of the People in London.* 17 vols. London: Williams and Norgate.

Clayton, O., Jr., ed. 1995. *An American Dilemma Revisited: Race Relations in a Changing World.* New York: Russell Sage Foundation.

Deegan, M. J. 1985. Sociology at Wellesley College: 1900–1919. *History of Sociology* 6: 91–115.

Durkheim, E. 1933. *The Division of Labor in Society.* Glencoe, Ill.: Free Press.

———. 1960. *Suicide.* Glencoe, Ill.: Free Press.

Fish, V. K. 1985. Hull House: Pioneer in urban research during its creative years. *History of Sociology* 6: 32–53.

Foote, N. N., and L. S. Cottrell, Jr. 1958. *Identity and Interpersonal Competence: A New Direction in Family Research.* Chicago: University of Chicago Press.

Gitlin, T. 1995. Sociology for whom? Criticism for whom? In *Sociology in America*, edited by H. Gans, 214–26. Newbury Park, Calif.: Sage.

Glass, John, and Jan M. Fritz. 1982. Clinical sociology: Origins and development. *Clinical Sociology Review* 1: 3–6.

Gouldner, A. 1970. *The Coming Crisis in Western Sociology.* New York: Basic Books.

Johnson, C. S. 1922. *The Negro in Chicago: A Study of Race Relations and a Race Riot.* Chicago: University of Chicago Press.

Larson, C. J. 1993. *Pure and Applied Sociological Theory: Problems and Issues.* Ft. Worth, Tex.: Harcourt Brace Jovanovich.

Lazersfeld, P., B. Berelson, and H. Gaudet. 1948. *The People's Choice.* New York: Columbia University Press.

Marx, K. 1867. *Capital.* Vol. 1. Moscow: Foreign Languages Press.

Marx, K., and F. Engels. 1955. *The Communist Manifesto.* Edited by S. H. Beer. New York: Appleton-Century-Crofts.

Olsen, M. 1992. What is sociological practice? *Sociological Practice Review* 3, no. 1 (January): 50–51.

Peck, A. 1985. *The Sixties: The Life and Times of the Underground Press.* New York: Pantheon Books.

Pettigrew, T. F., ed. 1980. *The Sociology of Race Relations.* New York: Free Press.

Robbins, R. 1997. *Sidelines Activist: Charles S. Johnson and the Struggle for Civil Rights.* Jackson, Miss.: University of Mississippi Press.

Smelser, N. J. 1994. *Sociology.* Cambridge, Mass.: Blackwell.

Stouffer, S. A. 1949. *The American Soldier.* 2 vols. Princeton, N.J.: Princeton University Press.

Thomas, W. I., and F. Znaniecki. 1918–1920. *The Polish Peasant in Europe and America.* Chicago: The University of Chicago Press.

Ward, L. F. 1906. *Applied Sociology: A Treatise on the Conscious Improvement of Society.* Boston: Ginn.

———. 1883. *Dynamic Sociology.* 2 vols. New York: Appleton.

———. 1903. *Pure Sociology.* New York: Macmillan.

Weber, M. 1958. *The Protestant Ethic and the Spirit of Capitalism.* New York: Scribners.

Wirth, L. 1931. Clinical sociology. *American Journal of Sociology* 37: 49–66.

Zetterberg, H. L. 1956. *Sociology in the United States of America.* Paris, France: UNESCO. Reprint, Westport, Conn.: Greenwood Press, 1973.

SUPPLEMENTAL READING

Bulmer, M. 1985. This Chicago School of Sociology: What made it a school? *History of Sociology* 5: 60–115.

Comte, A. 1957. *A General View of Positivism.* New York: Robert Speller and Sons.

Desmond, A., and J. Moore. 1991. *Darwin: The Life of a Tormented Evolutionist.* New York: W. W. Norton.

Durkheim, E. 1938. *The Rules of the Sociological Method.* Glencoe, Ill.: Free Press.

Gerth, H., and C. W. Mills, eds. 1958. *From Max Weber: Essays in Sociology.* New York: Oxford University Press.

Larson, C. J. 1986. *Sociological Theory from the Enlightenment to the Present.* Bayside, N.Y.: General Hall.

Lukes, S. 1972. *Emile Durkheim; His Life and Work, a Historical and Critical Study.* New York: Harper & Row.

Odum, H. W., ed. 1927. *American Masters of Social Science.* New York: Henry Holt.

Padover, S. K. 1978. *Karl Marx: An Intimate Biography.* New York: McGraw-Hill.

Park, R. E., and E. W. Burgess. 1922. *Introduction to the Science of Society.* Chicago: University of Chicago Press.

Spencer, H. 1880. *First Principles.* Vol. 1. New York: A. L. Burt.

Steele, S. F., and J. M. Iutcovich, eds. 1997. *Directions in Applied Sociology: Presidential Addresses of the Society for Applied Sociology.* Arnold, Md.: Society for Applied Sociology.

Sumner, W. G. 1960. *Folkways.* New York: Mentor.

Weber, M. 1974. *Max Weber: A Biography.* New York: Wiley.

2

Notes on Theory

INTRODUCTION

As pointed out in chapter 1, the domain of sociological practice remains muddled. To a large extent, the increasing numbers of sociologists who work in practice settings find themselves in uncharted waters. They have been taught in university sociology programs that often continue to follow Ogburn's 1929 advice to the discipline: be interested "in one thing only, to wit, discovering new knowledge" (Pettigrew 1980, xxii). Their training has seldom given them the capacity to use their sociology except in teaching. Quite the contrary: the training they have received often amounts to "trained incapacity," that is, training that tends to incapacitate them and others from using their sociological knowledge. These sociologists in practice settings who are without practice training must invent their own ways of putting sociology into action. They often are forced to draw from practice fields outside of sociology, such as social work or community psychology.

Such strategies to some degree inevitably compromise the sociological orientation of the interventions they design. Sometimes, though, sociologists in practice settings who lack practice training invent ways of putting their sociology into action patterns that are true to the sociological paradigms of the discipline. By building upon the pioneering innovations of practicing sociologists who had to devise their own ways of "enacting" sociology, this book takes a step toward a time when sociologists who wish to practice will have available more guidance from within the field about how to put their learning to use.

The application of each science turns upon the foundational wheel of a theory. A theory in a science is a logically interrelated set of propositions about empirical reality. The most frequently used metaphor for a social theory is that it is a lens through which a social scientist observes social phenomena. The latter cannot be perceived or recorded without the use of a lens, whether the scientist is conscious of this or not. A social theory ranges from a small, partial concept that is an implicit part of a larger whole to a series of concepts so sweeping as to encompass whole societies. Macro-social theories account for societal stability and dynamics, for conflict and upheaval, and indeed for the rise and fall of whole civilizations. Micro-social theories, in contrast, enable us to interpret the effects of groups on individual behavior and the process of interpersonal behavior. One should remember, too, that all social theories are more or less abstract. Some provide lenses so close to grounded reality as to enable the tracking of ants, whereas others are fitted to the highest imaginable altitude needed for viewing an entire system of ecological and technological events (such as globalization, for example).

Social theories utilized by sociological practitioners are seldom made highly explicit in their conferences, encounters with clients, and reports. This is equally true of physical engineers and physicians. In principle, the findings from practice might well draw deliberately from theory and should often contribute to strengthening theories—but this is seldom the case. That clients are usually suspicious of and somewhat antagonistic toward theoretical assumptions explains this in part.

Perhaps the most influential academic sociologist of the 1940s and 1950s, Talcott Parsons, devoted nearly all of his professional energies to the development of a comprehensive theory of social systems and subsystems (Parsons 1949, 1960). He elaborated upon a functional frame of reference grounded in what Emile Durkheim had defined as social facts, arguing that society is a kind of organism that must adapt to environmental circumstances, and that it contains the micro-social facts of individual behaviors that show parallel forms of adaptation. The relevant question to be addressed by the sociologist within this framework, then, is that of what adaptive functions are being served by the observed behavior. This is functionalist theory. Its altitude was high and its terminology abstract. Parsons's version of it was unsuited to applied work, which he regarded as a questionable, even undesirable use of sociological energies in any event; he wrote that we do not yet know enough about the structure and functioning of society to enable us to make informed and durable interventions.

One of his students, Robert K. Merton (1967), carried on the functionalist tradition far into the 1980s. Merton occasionally engaged in applied work and his conceptual formulations hovered at what he called the "middle range," being more accessible to and useful for practitioners. His theories have played a part in applied formulations of social problems and in causal models used in some program evaluations.

Alternative theoretical frameworks—most notably conflict or coercion theory in Ralf Dahrendorf (1959) and Lewis A. Coser (1956), and in Europe, critical theory—abound in academic sociology. Indeed, Marxian interpretations live on as a kind of conceptual subset in the field. Exchange theory, a crossover from economics, became highly fashionable in the 1980s, under the influence of James Coleman. For all of this, symbolic interactionism is the most commonly used frame of reference in sociological practice. As I shall show, it has stood the test of time, continues to be refined, and fits the needs and interests of sociotherapists, community organizers, social planners, and many program evaluators.

SYMBOLIC INTERACTIONISM

Functionalist and system theories tended strongly in their heyday to move at a level of abstraction that did not include everyday social life and the feelings of individuals. They also paid relatively little attention to marginal and subdominant groups. Symbolic interactionism, born in the 1920s and 1930s (as noted in chapter 1), was revived during the 1960s as a kind of antidote to the impersonal qualities of Parsonian theories. Interactionism gives major emphasis to the proposition that humans behave in response to the meanings that events and groups and significant other persons have for them, and that these meanings—themselves the product of social interaction—are more varied and complex interpretively than they are matters of conformity to role expectations.

The approach I propose draws from a theoretical and methodological framework that lies well within the American sociological tradition of symbolic, or interpretive, interactionism (cf. Blumer 1969; Denzin 1989). In terms of methodology, I advocate a research approach. As such, our approach is consistent with and draws from what has been the predominant orientation taught in university sociology programs since the 1920s. That is, we draw from and utilize the aspect of Ogburn's orientation which says that sociologists are social scientists with skills in discovery of knowledge about social groups. University programs in sociological practice must continue to provide strong training in research methods. However, training in an additional type of research method is needed: a type of research method capable of simultaneously generating sociological knowledge and translating that knowledge into problem-responsive action. What is needed is the research method advocated in this book as a basic element of sociological practice rooted in interpretive interactionism: *participatory research* (see Whyte 1991, 9). In participatory research, informants become active participants in the research along with the sociologists. The approach is one in which sociologists and clients become collaborators: co-problem assessors and co-problem solvers.

When I say that participatory research should be incorporated across the board in the activities of practicing sociologists, I am not saying that "one size fits all." As will be seen from the case examples in this book, there is great variety in the research approaches that practicing sociologists have devised. The approaches range from those where sociologists work with formal committees of stakeholders in local organizations, communities, and larger organized bodies to those where sociologists work informally with families or individuals to collaboratively develop and test hypotheses about problems.

Whyte's Participatory Action Research (PAR) project with Xerox Corporation (Whyte 1991, ch. 2) is an example of a participatory research approach to practicing sociology in a large organization. The practicing sociologists successfully worked with a formal stakeholders' committee on the problem of how to save $3.2 million and retain 180 jobs. Simmons's use of Grounded Therapy is an example of a participatory research approach to practicing sociology with individuals (Simmons 1994). Working informally with the individual client as a co-researcher, Simmons constructs a preconception-free grounded theory (Glaser and Strauss 1967) of the therapy client's self-defined problem and a plan of therapeutic action for the client. Though very different in many aspects, a significant commonality of both Whyte's PAR and Simmons's Grounded Therapy is that they are both research approaches to practicing sociology.

FIVE FEATURES OF THE APPROACH

This section identifies five aspects of the research-based interactionist approach that are important to understanding the significance of this approach. These are:

1. ways this approach strengthens the professional self-confidence and credibility of individual practicing sociologists
2. ways the quality of theories in sociology could potentially be improved by the approach
3. changes in society that may increase receptivity to this kind of sociological practice
4. ways in which the dynamics of the social situation created by using this approach are conducive to producing social change
5. implications and consequences of the fact that the participatory approach exposes practitioners to the sociopolitical contexts surrounding the problems in which they are trying to intervene.

Each of these aspects of the research-based interactionist approach to practicing sociology is briefly discussed here, in hopes that the reader will be able to identify them operating in the experiences of the practitioners profiled in case examples throughout this book.

Professional Confidence and Credibility

The first aspect of the approach is that, in my view, sociologists who use it do not have to go through the common experience of "identity abandonment" or disidentification when they enter practice. This is signalled by the tendency of sociologists in practice settings to describe themselves using occupational titles other than "sociologist." They do so because the prevailing view is that sociologists have nothing practical to offer; that they engage only in the pursuit of "pure" knowledge (i.e., knowledge with no immediate practical use). This, of course, is exactly the view cultivated by Ogburn and his latter-day adherents who continue to dominate the discipline of sociology.

I believe that practicing sociologists who adopt the participatory research-based interactionist approach will be less shy about embracing the label *sociologist*. They will be able to identify with their academic roots, and at the same time show the usefulness of those roots as they establish research partnerships with their clients. They move beyond the role of the "value-free" (read: aloof and superior) academician who does research by putting research subjects (read: subordinates) under a microscope. The interactionist practitioner has received the academic sociological training in theory and research methods, but makes the transition into applying them with a participatory approach. It is hoped that this transition can be facilitated by a training program designed around the assumption that discovering knowledge and making the world a better place are compatible pursuits.

Improvement in Quality of Theories

The second aspect of sociological practice, based on participatory research and guided by interactionist theory, is that it has the potential to contribute to better integrated theory in the discipline of sociology. Particularly if focused and supported by a consortium of associations (such as the Society for Applied Sociology, the Sociological Practice Association, the Sociological Practice Section of the American Sociological Association, and the Committee on Practice, Applied, and Clinical Sociology of the Pacific Sociological Association), sociological practice may create increasingly integrated theories as part of the work of doing sociology.

Within such a consortium of associations built on practice, theorists might come into their own. Serviceable middle-range theories summarizing principles of social structures, societal development and change (on the one hand), and micro-social features of group behavior and interpersonal relations (on the other hand) can be formulated as opening guidelines for the knowledge base of practice. Branches could build outward from each of these two trunks, each providing statements of key concepts in each of the main domains of practice. Theorists could occupy themselves fruitfully as well, by keeping up with the flow of applied and clinical literature, extracting therefrom the most promising and prospectively generic ideas and assumptions that undergird the findings from and challenges facing practitioners. These men and women would be drawn from both the sociologist and practitioner "sides" of participatory research partnerships (cf. Dentler 1995, 11–12).

Societal Acceptance of Sociological Practice

Third, the time may be right for widespread acceptance of this approach to practice, based on partnerships between sociologists and clients that are focused on collaborative, problem-oriented inquiry. There has been a dramatic growth of support for collaborative policies and programs from the local to the international level. As Rosalyn Benjamin Darling (1996, 135) wrote, "Human services today are increasingly coming to be based on a 'partnership' model in which service users and service providers have equal status. This model is replacing the 'professional dominance' model that prevailed in the past." It may be hypothesized that in this transitional period referred to by Darling there will be more widespread adoption of the new partnership model among service users than among service providers. In such circumstances, those service professionals, such as sociologists using the participatory research approach, who adopt the new partnership model will have an advantage in competition for service users over those service professionals and professions who continue to adhere to the old professional dominance model.

Mark and Joyce Iutcovich (1987) have argued that sociological practice as a field must become entrepreneurial if it is to grow. They say we must be mobilized and ready to respond as a professional community to any opportunities that present themselves. I believe this admonition should be taken in light of the preceding assessment that there is currently more user demand than provider supply for the partnership approach to professional services. There is now an opportunity for the sociological practice profession to grow through entrepreneurial action by the professional community. Widespread adoption of this approach to practicing sociology, based on partnerships between sociologists and clients focused on collaborative, problem-oriented inquiry, may be the entrepreneurial thing to do.

Producing Social Change

Fourth, theoretical principles and empirical findings from social psychology suggest that an approach like the one described here is potentially effective for inducing problem-responsive change in group social structures and cultures. There is support from social psychology both for the "intervention outcome" in our approach (inducing problem-responsive actions through inquiry) and for the method by which this outcome is sought (partnerships between sociologists and clients). First, there is support for both features of the intervention outcome: that it is focused on changing actions and that it attempts to do so through information-seeking inquiry. The focus on problem-responsive action is consistent with Deutscher's suggestion, in a landmark work (Deutscher, Pestello, and Pastel 1993), that the basis for change in social reality is change in peoples' actions. People's actions flow not from their individual attitudes, but rather from their collectively defined situations. Changed patterns of human activity flow from changes in socially defined situations.

The focus on inquiry as a basis for building actions that effectively respond to problems is supported by R. W. White's theory about information assimilation and levels of adaptation (White 1974; cf. Golan 1981). Those who engage in problem-solving activity most competently, White suggested, are those at the "mastery" level of adaptation. Their ability to respond effectively to problems results from their ability to assimilate (i.e., take in and make sense of) a maximum amount of information about their environments. At the other extreme, the most maladaptive actions are done by those at the "defensive" level of adaptation. They lack accurate and predictive "cognitive maps" of their environments and cannot assimilate information about important features of their environment. Therefore, they engage in defensive action strategies that "screen out" unexpected, undesired, unchosen, ill-understood aspects of their environments. Unfocused aggressive and passively aggressive (as opposed to assertive) activities, retreatist responses (including clinical depression at the extreme), and obsessive behavior patterns all qualify as defensive.

The approach to practicing sociology discussed here uses orderly yet user-friendly research methods to gather information about problematic situations. The information is therefore likely to be assimilated rather than defensively screened out by the participants. Such an approach tends to generate effective responses to problems; that is, responses that White called "competently adaptative."

A fair amount of theory and research in social psychology points to the particular effectiveness of the method of sociologists and clients acting together as equals to solve common problems. This approach appears conducive to creating a socially defined situation and set of activities that could be described as "collective buy-in." Three especially important social psychological factors, among numerous others, operate to create collective buy-in:

1. the presence of superordinate goals that create a sense of interdependence among the participants
2. equality of social status among the participants, which gives each a sense of valued contribution to the group

3. a shared sense of freedom from constraint among participants, which reduces their resistance to the forward flow of collective activity (Stephan and Stephan 1990, chs. 1, 2, and 10; Fisher 1982, ch. 2)

Thus, there are reasons, rooted in social psychology, to believe that this approach has the potential to result in "partner" relationships between sociologists and clients, which relations can be expected to produce social change. The approach is focused on supporting development of competent action plans and scenarios that the participants buy into based on interdependence in the pursuit of superordinate goals, status equality among the participants, and participants' perception that their actions are voluntary rather than externally constrained or coerced.

Sociopolitical Contexts

The fifth feature of the participatory research approach to practicing sociology might be termed sociopolitical. All practicing sociologists (those using a participatory research approach as well as others) are closer to and more affected by the sociopolitical interplay of multiple participants on various "sides" of the problems and social issues they address than are academic sociologists. However, users of the participatory research approach have what R.W. White (1974) would call a more competently adaptative understanding of the multiple standpoints and perspectives of people making up the structure of an organization, community, family, or other social whole than do either traditional academic sociologists or other practicing sociologists.

Those doing traditional academic sociology often are not sensitive to or significantly affected by this issue because they screen out the actual activities of the people in the social contexts they study. Frequently the data they deal with are only statistical, so they see only the forest and not the trees. Those doing other forms of applied sociology tend to be in contact with a more limited range of stakeholders than are participatory research practitioners; thus, in their own way they also effectively screen out the full range of perspectives. For example, as program evaluators they have contact only with a few members of top management; as community organizers they may have little contact with persons outside of the dispossessed group they are organizing for conflict; as therapists they may deal with only one individual.

There are two potentially contradictory outcomes of exposure to the perspectives of a wide range of stakeholders through using this research-oriented participatory approach. On the one hand, drawing from the symbolic interactionist theory on which the approach is based, the sociologist makes a conscious effort to understand the standpoints and perspectives of different types of participants in the targeted social setting. This gives the sociologist a greater understanding of the complexity of factors that retard change in social contexts than would other approaches. Each stakeholder's perspective may be based on a "vested interest" that she or he sees as threatened by impending change, leading to resistance. Understanding this potential can aid the practicing sociologist in planning for superordinate goals and equal-status partnerships to knit together various stakeholders into a more unified, action-ready set.

On the other hand, participative contact with members located at different vantage points in a social setting has its risks. This is especially so when there are no efforts to link stakeholder groups into more unified action-sets that include the sociologist, or when such efforts are ineffective. Becker, in an article titled, "Whose Side Are We On?" (1967), explained two related kinds of risks for sociologists generally, which I believe are particular risks for practicing sociologists. He stated that the risks are greatest when groups have defined their relationships with each other in politicized, adversarial terms. Especially in such situations, the sociologist will tend to become biased or be accused of bias. *Bias* means falling into sympathy with one side in a many-sided situation, and as a result, sociologically buying into and telling that side's story while neglecting or distorting the perspectives of the other stakeholders.

Although Peter Rossi does not use a participatory research approach to practice, he does engage in applied research (an important area of generic sociological practice). In an article titled, "No Good Applied Social Research Goes Unpunished" (1987) Rossi relates an experience that illustrates the second category of risk identified by Becker. Rossi did unbiased research on homelessness, for which he was nevertheless punished by being accused of bias by a members of a stakeholder group, homeless advocates.

Before telling this story, however, Rossi identifies important additional stakeholder groups within the discipline of sociology that relate to the issue now under discussion. He notes that practicing sociologists are also likely to be denigrated by the dominant, academically oriented groups in their own discipline. Reacting to the sting of such denigration, he writes that his own "applied research has certainly not been motivated by earning brownie points or merit pay. Among members of my discipline, applied research ranks far behind the writing of opaque exegeses on the writings of long-deceased social commentators whose works would (according to my lights) best be allowed to dissolve into obscurity" (74).

Moving on to his main story, Rossi explains his nonbiased and technically competent studies of the number of homeless in Chicago, which showed a homeless population of about one-tenth the size of the estimate made by the Chicago Homeless Coalition. The latter were a major pro-homeless stakeholder group. From their perspective, they had a vested interest in there being a much larger number of homeless persons in Chicago. Acting consistently with their perspective, they subjected Rossi's report "to a torrent of criticism, ranging from the purely technical to the accusation of having sold out to the conservative forces of the Reagan administration and the Thompson Illinois regime. The major theme was that our report had seriously damaged the cause of homeless people in Chicago by providing state and local officials with an excuse to dismiss the problem as trivial" (79), though Rossi says that services were actually increased as a result of his research. Further, Rossi says he was subject to "the longest stretch of personal abuse I have suffered since basic training in the Army during World War II" (79).

Rossi has put his finger on a major issue for the field of practicing sociology, a major problematic feature of the situations in which practicing sociologists work. Sociologists experience a unique form of what E. V. Stonequist (1937), Everett Hughes (1949), and Robert Merton (1957) have called marginality. *Marginality* is the situation of one who uses a group as a reference group—that is, adopts the perspective of the group and expects or desires status in the group—but is either not accepted by or is outright degraded by the group. She or he is pushed to the margins of the group. The experience described by Rossi, which represents a common pattern of experiences among practicing sociologists, is really a problem in their role-sets (Merton 1957, 368–84) which we call *double marginality*. Practicing sociologists desire status in the discipline of sociology as well as among member stakeholder groups in the social contexts where they practice. Often, though, they experience nonacceptance or degradation by both; they experience double marginality.

Arguments for the Research-Based Interactionist Approach

In sum, an approach to practice that is rooted in interactionist theory and guided by participatory research has much to recommend it. Such an approach allows full expression of our professional identities and utilization of our methodological and analytical skills. Further, its use can potentially enrich sociological theory. Additionally, the time is probably right for widespread adoption of the approach, because it is compatible with the new partnership model of relationship between service providers and users. A very important fourth reason for using this approach is that its social psychological dynamics are conducive to producing changed definitions of situations and activity patterns, which are the stuff of social structural and cultural change.

The most important reason for adopting an approach to practicing sociology based on inquiry-focused partnerships between sociologists and clients has to do with the sociopolitical aspect of the situations in which practicing sociologists work. This approach allows the practitioner to effectively assess and respond to sources of resistance to change when the resistance is rooted in vested interests. Using this approach, tools can be fashioned to respond effectively to (or even avoid) the double marginality commonly experienced by practicing sociologists. Sociologist-client partnerships, created in the participatory research process and buttressed by strong peer support through our professional associations, can enable us to function at the mastery level in the sociopolitical contexts of our work.

Mainstream sociology experienced sociopolitical marginality at the turn of the twentieth century when mainstream sociologists were actively engaged in social reform. The discipline adapted defensively to these role-set problems by retreating from reform into a sole focus on the pursuit of new knowledge. I believe that the field of practicing sociology, using tools forged with the collaborative inquiry approach and spearheaded by the practicing sociology consortium of professional associations, will ultimately lead mainstream sociology out of its defensive retreatism. Sociology as a whole will then experience adaptive mastery in practicing sociology in a work situation where change-oriented practice is welcomed.

THE CHICAGO SCHOOL AND THE INVENTION OF SYMBOLIC INTERACTIONISM AMIDST A RETREAT FROM SOCIAL REFORM

Symbolic interactionism may be considered the premier American sociological approach for the study of and, potentially, effective response to social problems. Symbolic interactionism was invented in the laboratory of social problems: Chicago in the 1900–1930 period, at the University of Chicago Sociology Department.

As Ritzer (1993) pointed out, departments and faculty at the University of Chicago were expected to do original thinking and research and to publish their results; at the same time, they were encouraged to do public service and to be involved in what was taking place in the city of Chicago. In an inventive response to these twin, and potentially competing, university policies, the sociology department adopted the view that "[t]he city of Chicago is one of the most complete social laboratories in the world. . . . No city in the world presents a wider variety of typical social problems than Chicago" (Fitzgerald 1990, 41). With this orientation, the Chicago sociologists were "satisfying the demands of the university to do innovative work and to be involved in the community and were simultaneously doing the kind of work that would further their own careers as well as the field of sociology" (Ritzer 1993, 71).

Symbolic interactionism was created as the Chicago approach to simultaneously assimilating information about the complexity of social problems through research and responding to social problems through community involvement. This framework, which is both a theory and a method, grew out of intensive study of the social problems of Chicago. As Becker (1966) wrote, out of the detailed examination of the community context in which these problems existed, symbolic interactionism emerged to systematize and make sense of the real-life observations. Graduate students were, for example, advised as follows:

You have been told to go grubbing in the library, thereby accumulating a mass of notes and a liberal coating of grime. You have been told to choose problems wherever you find musty stacks of routine records based on trivial schedules prepared by tired bureaucrats and filled out by reluctant applicants for aid or fussy do-gooders or indifferent clerks. This is called "getting your hands dirty in social research." Those who counsel you are wise and honorable; the reasons they offer are of great value. But one more thing is needful: first-hand observation. Go and sit in the lounges of the luxury hotels and on the doorsteps of the flophouses; sit on the Gold Coast settees and on the slum shakedowns; sit in the Orchestra Hall and in the Star and Garter Burlesk. In short, gentlemen, go get the seat of your pants dirty in real research. (Park, cited in Bulmer 1984, 97)

The research method of "participant observation," often coupled with informal interviewing, soon became a key entry in the catalogue of methods developed by the early Chicago School sociologists to investigate social life on a first-hand basis. The method is also an early recipe for establishing the research-based sociologist-client partnership that is at the core of our inquiry approach to practicing sociology.

The first of a major line of studies of social problem topics, done by Chicago School graduate students using the method called participant observation, was Nels Anderson's study, *The Hobo* (1923). Anderson was not a typical participant observer; the usual would have been an academic sociologist who entered a "native" social world (Ritzer 1993, 98). But Anderson was a logical candidate to be the person who defined this new methodology, because at the beginning his primary role and identity were not those of an academic sociologist. He was in fact a hobo attempting to move out of that way of life by doing this study as part of becoming certified as an academic sociologist. Thus, he was well suited to fulfill the most important requirement of this kind of research: gaining access to the world being studied. As he said:

I did not descend into the pit, assume a role there, and later ascend to brush off the dust. I was in the process of moving out of the hobo world. To use a hobo expression, preparing the book was a way of "getting by," earning a living while the exit was under way. The role was familiar before the research began. (Anderson, cited in Bulmer 1984, 98)

Because of his comfortable familiarity with the culture and social structure of the social world of hobos, Anderson was readily able to establish rapport with hobos. Note how his obvious familiarity with the social rules of the hobo world allowed him to invent a system for establishing the trust relationships necessary to conduct high-quality informal interviews (and thereby to do good research!):

I began with informal interviews, sitting with a man on the curb, sitting in the lobby of a hotel or a flop house, going with someone for a cup of coffee with doughnut or rolls. I had to develop some system for these interviews, as I had to devise some system in writing them down. . . .

I discovered that one sitting next to someone else can effectively start conversation by thinking out loud. It invites attention and one needs but to come out of his reveries, tell of the thought in mind. One must avoid causing those approached to feel that he is after something; the price of a beer, a cup of coffee or a meal. One must expect to do some spending but must keep at the level of frugal spending. (Anderson, cited in Ritzer 1993, 98)

This ability to establish relationships of trust in participant observation, based on familiarity with members' folkways about demonstrating trustworthiness, is crucial for more than good research. I think this key ingredient in participant observation is also the basic requirement for creating the problem-solving partnerships that are essential in the participatory research approach to practicing sociology. Participant observation is, of course, a research method. Those who use it are not necessarily also practicing sociology by engaging in participatory problem solving. I think, though, that invention of the method of participant observation in the Chicago School should be seen as a critical step toward creation of this symbolic interactionist approach to practicing sociology. Derived from the emerging symbolic interactionist perspective, participant observation with and informal interviewing of members of "social problem worlds" was devised as a way of telling the stories of community underdogs from their own points of view.

Translation of participant observational research into problem-responsive action, in ways respectful of members' stories, is a logical next derivative of symbolic interactionism. I will argue that the rise of symbolic interactionism should be viewed in the context of a general retreat from social reform by the men of the Chicago School, a retreat prompted by the sociopolitical situation in the city of Chicago and the nation. However, the retreat of the symbolic interactionists was unlike that of the other major Chicago group, the urban ecologists and their champions like Ogburn. The latter moved into a "value-free" social science theoretical framework, where they disengaged from the stakeholders making up the sociopolitical situation in the city. In their retreat, the symbolic interactionists invented a perspective that was the metaphoric equivalent of a behind-the-lines staging area. From this conceptual staging area, a new social-science-based strategy for reform could be organized—one based on engagement with the stakeholders making up the sociopolitical context.

The symbolic interactionist framework grew up from intensive study of the social problems of Chicago. As Becker (1966) said, out of detailed examination of the community context in which these problems existed, symbolic interactionism emerged to systematize and make sense of the real-life observations. The picture that emerged, and that came to be formalized in the theoretical framework called "symbolic interactionism" (Blumer 1969) is that of individual actors (including groups as well as persons) imbedded in symbolic, or interpretive, interaction with others. *Symbolic* and *interpretive* in relation to interaction refer to the fact that actors are constantly engaged in a process of mentally, or cognitively, interpreting the meaning of each others' actions by symbolically categorizing them, and acting toward others based on

the meanings assigned to the others. These meanings and actions are iden-
tity-based. Individual actors' actions toward each other are based on their
cognitive appraisals of their own identities in relationship to that of the others.

From this standpoint, the social problems of the city, such as homelessness
or delinquency, are the product of "interactional careers." Delinquency, for
example, arises from delinquent careers in a process by which individuals
become delinquent through being appraised by others and through self-ap-
praisal as "delinquent." From the symbolic interactionist perspective, effective responses to the delinquency problem should be directed at changing the
"shape" of delinquents' interactional careers; that is, at making their careers
more conventional.

Chicago School sociologist Clifford Shaw (1931), for example, developed
an approach to modifying delinquent careers, which revolved around the delinquents' own stories of their delinquent careers. The approach is a good
example of an early practice technique created in the symbolic interactionist
staging area. It builds a bridge from interviewing and participant observational research to participatory problem-responsive action. Through mutual
empathy built up by the democratic sharing inherent in the methods used for
drawing out the delinquent's life story, Shaw and his client would create a
situation of collective buy-in, which, as noted earlier, this type of approach is
good at producing. The youth was motivated to set a new life-career agenda.
Through understanding of the youth's own perspective on his world and on
the turning points in his life career, Shaw was able to identify conventional
roles that were compatible with deviant roles the youth had incorporated into
his personality earlier in life.

For example, in the case study of a delinquent youth named Stanley, Shaw
was able to see that the conventional occupation of commercial salesman might
be suitable. Stanley's deep aversion to taking orders, acquired earlier by embracing of a variety of roles in nonconventional social worlds (e.g., the under-
world and a correctional facility he called "the house of corruption"), could
be accommodated in this occupation:

As a salesman in the field, he took orders only from himself and was not liable to
correction from others. His personality traits of attractive manners, his forcible and
logical presentation of points, and his ability to make friends were positive assets in
his new vocation. (Shaw 1931, 196)

As noted in the previous chapter, the impulse toward sociological practice defined as social reform was widespread among American sociologists in the early 1900s. This was particularly true at the University of Chicago, where reform-oriented sociology centered around the work of Jane Addams at Hull House and her male and female sociological colleagues (Deegan 1986). However, reform-oriented sociologists soon began to experience the double marginality that practicing sociologists continue to face today. They were attacked by the business and other elites of Chicago (notably and prominently Standard Oil interests) who perceived that their vested interests were threatened by the reforms the sociologists sought. The reformers were likewise discredited by their colleagues at the university who saw them as unacademic moralists.

Major displacements of key reform-oriented sociologists occurred as mainstream sociology retreated from social reform, both in Chicago and throughout the United States. Jane Addams was snubbed both by many of her sociological colleagues and by the elites. She responded by moving into the development of the new discipline of social work. Bemis, Zeublin, and Thomas, all eminent reformist members of the early Chicago School, were forced out of the university. By 1918 (during the Red Scare), the only representatives of the early Chicago reformist sociologists remaining were George Herbert Mead and Albion Small (Deegan 1986, 314).

Chicago sociology (and American sociology, because Chicago sociology was the trendsetter) was now faced with a situation of role conflict, which was succinctly summed up by Ernest Becker as a "tension between these two poles: the human urgency of the social problem on the one end and the quiet respectability of objective science on the other" (Becker 1971, 6). Two groups of Chicago sociologists adapted to this situation in fundamentally different ways. The urban ecologists, headed by Robert E. Park and Ernest Burgess, devised what we have termed a defensive adaptational strategy. They rejected one horn of the dilemma described by Ernest Becker and embraced the other; in essence, they ignored the human urgency of social problems and devoted themselves to the quiet respectability of objective science.

Park, for example, was known for strongly advocating that sociology should distance itself from social reform. There is, in fact, a strong undercurrent of antagonism toward those who try to address social problems directly through their sociology. Although Park himself had shown strong reformist inclinations in his years as a journalist, he changed as he became an academic, and often went as far as to sarcastically deride reformists. For example, one of the historians of the Chicago School said that "[m]ore than once he drove students to anger or tears by such reproofs as 'You're another one of those damn do-gooders' " (Faris 1967, 32). In what I see as an overreaction to the criticism—from both within and outside of the university—that the earlier Chicago sociologists like Jane Addams were unacademic moralists, Park once said, "A moral man cannot be a sociologist" (quoted in Matthews 1977, 17). Park's view was that

[i]n developing the techniques of sociology we must escape both HISTORY and PRACTICAL APPLICATIONS. . . . The first thing you have to do with a student is to show him that he can make a contribution if he doesn't try to improve anybody. . . . The trouble with our sociology in America is that it has had so much to do with churches and preachers. (Rauschenbush 1979, 97)

Ernest Burgess showed more ambivalence than Park. Early in his career he had been actively involved in social reform, and had even been a resident of Hull House, but during the 1920s he became more and more imbued with Park's anti-reform views. His autobiography (which never was finished) revealed his recognition of his own ambivalence in its title, *I Renounce Social Reform and Reformers: The Story of a Conflict of Social Roles* (Deegan 1986, 145). The theme of the book was intended to be that it is not possible for sociologists both to generate and teach the knowledge of the science of society and to be engaged in the practice of action to resolve social problems. Burgess believed that there should be a division of labor between the knowledge generators (sociologists) and the knowledge appliers (social workers).

In contrast, the symbolic interactionists built and traveled on a different road toward resolution of the double marginality of sociological practice. They did not follow the "role-segregation" pathway blazed by Park and Burgess. The symbolic interactionists' project moves toward resolution of the "social problem versus social science" conflict through collaborative *unification* of social research and social practice. It is a project inherited from and continuing the work of Jane Addams at Hull House (Deegan 1986).

Addams and her sociological colleagues rejected the notion of social science subscribed to by Park and Burgess, in which sociologists acted as outside experts who analyzed the social problem-carrying populations of the city as though they were specimens in a social laboratory. Hull House was guided by a philosophy in which sociologists worked collaboratively with neighborhood residents, who were viewed as experts about their own neighborhoods. Addams said:

I have always objected to the phrase "sociological laboratory" applied to us [at Hull House], because Settlements should be something much more human and spontaneous than such a phrase connotes, and yet it is inevitable that the residents should know their own neighborhoods more thoroughly than any other, and that their experience there should affect their convictions. (cited in Deegan 1986, 35)

Based on this collaborative vision of social science, Hull House sociologists, professionals, and working-class neighborhood residents invented what were, in effect, social research and problem-solving teams. They gathered statistical and participant observational information about the needs of the surrounding neighborhoods, summarized in such documents as *Hull House Maps and Papers* (Addams 1895). These teams formed what Mead called "working hypotheses" about the sources of problematic neighborhood conditions. Then, policies and action plans were collaboratively formed and carried out. The resulting Hull House programs included a branch of the public library, an art gallery, clubs, classes, a coffee house, a gymnasium, a kindergarten, a nursery, a music school, a theater, a women's cooperative apartment, a men's club, and a men's residence, among others. Symbolic interactionists such as William I. Thomas and George Herbert Mead maintained close ties with Jane Addams and Hull House, participating in many of its activities. Their intellectual project, symbolic interactionism, I believe, should be seen as a metaphorical staging area for the further invention of approaches for responding to social problems in ways that, like the Hull House efforts, collaboratively unify sociological research and sociological practice.

The way symbolic interactionism does this is by formalizing the central insight on which the Hull House approach was based. This insight recognizes that the approach of the outside-expert, value-free sociologists (like Park, Burgess, Ogburn, and their present-day followers) will not yield effective responses to social problems. The sociologist must enter into and become part of the community in order to understand and to promote change in it.

For symbolic interactionists, social problems result from collective definitions of certain social situations as problematic. These definitions of situations can only be understood and changed from within, by participatively entering into and thereby understanding and then helping modify the cogni-

tive and communicative process that led to the collective recognition of the
problem. Mead's general perspective was that

conflict in society occurred when people were unable to take each other's "roles." The
remedy to social problems became more open communication. "Scientific information" collected in an "objective" manner provided a mechanism to understand the
issues involved in any given problem. All the participants in the dilemma could then
listen to and understand the different perspectives and situations. Since people were
rational beings and desired a peaceful and sociable existence, social reform girded
with liberal values was the logical way to plan social change. (Deegan 1986, 107)

Mead wrote that there should be an ongoing process of collaboratively
developing, testing, and revising "working hypotheses" for social betterment.
This was, he said, a process through which science and scientists should enter
into democratic dialogue with other members of society, toward the development of a more "progressive" society. Deegan noted that in proposing this
public process of generating and testing working hypotheses, "Mead combined scientific ideas with everyday ideas about the world to solve social problems" (1986, 110).

In his various social reform activities in Chicago, Mead attempted to put
his ideas about a collaborative process of generating, testing, and revising
working hypotheses into action. For example, as part of a five-year study of
the needs of the Chicago Stockyards District, done in conjunction with the
University of Chicago Settlement, Mead and his colleague Charles Henderson
studied wages in the meat-packing companies. Mead and Henderson worked
collaboratively with the board of the University of Chicago Settlement and
with executives of the Armour and Swift meat-packing houses as the final
report was being prepared. The Armour and Swift executives expressed reser-
vations about the interpretation of some of the data in the draft of the final
report. They were concerned that the report suggested that their wages were
too low and led to poverty. Mead and Henderson, in response, agreed to include in the report data showing that Swift and Armour were paying wages
that were not out of line with the industry as a whole. After meetings with
the executives, Mead agreed to some further modifications in controversial
paragraphs, in response to the companies' concerns about an "unsympathetic
tone toward the packers" (Deegan 1986, 114).

The final report, which was not objected to by the Armour or the Swift
firms, nevertheless contained a striking critique of the meat packers' wage

policies. Some of the data presented showed that, according to a measure devised to calculate a "poverty level," $800 per year was a necessary minimum income for a family of five. In contrast, the report showed, the average family size in the district was 5.33, and the average income was only $634.80. It was clear from the report that, despite the implicit justification of Swift and Armour by an extensive comparison to other companies in the industry, families were able to survive only by such strategies as having mothers join the work force, pulling children out of school at an early age, taking in boarders, having all family members work for income, and enduring overcrowding, poverty, and ill health (Deegan 1986, 114).

POINTERS FOR CONTEMPORARY PATHFINDERS: OUTLINES OF A PARTNERSHIP APPROACH TO PRACTICING SOCIOLOGY

The first step toward practicing sociology is to resolve our Burgess-type role conflicts in a different way than he did and than most academic sociologists today continue to do. What Martin Buber called an "I-it" relationship with those studied must be replaced with an "I-thou," or participatory, relationship. The practicing sociologist departs from the view holding that truth and science flow from the social scientist to the community and society and not vice versa or reflexively. Rather, the sociologist cultivates a relationship with members of the groups where practice occurs, a relationship in which both sociologist and members value each other's knowledge.

This participatory type of relationship between sociologist and member, of course, was foreshadowed in the participant observational research of the Chicago School sociologists. But the relationship of participant observer to social world member, such as that illustrated by Anderson's relationship to the hobos he studied, does not go far enough. We need to cultivate what Mead was beginning to define: a relationship between practicing sociologist and member in which *action change* is the mutual goal.

A number of specific models of action-focused participatory research have been spawned since Mead's pioneering work. Among these are community and organizational psychologist Kurt Lewin's approach, called action research (Lewin 1946); organizational psychologist Chris Argyris's strategy, named action science (Argyris, Putnam, and Smith 1985); and a number of techniques created in the program evaluation field, such as Smith's evaluability assessment (Smith 1989) and Cousins's "participatory evaluation" method (Cousins 1996). Still, the best-known contributor in this area is a sociologist: William F. Whyte. Whyte is a recipient of the American Sociological Association Section on Sociological Practice Award for Outstanding Contributions to the Field. His letter accepting this award suggested that the participatory research approach to practicing sociology should be endorsed by the Section.

Whyte is important for understanding the development of the bridge between social science and sociological practice, which originated in the Chicago School. He received his doctorate from the University of Chicago Sociology Department in the early 1940s, after receiving his initial research training at Harvard from 1936–1940. His time at Chicago was one when the social-science-versus-social-problem tensions were still prominent. But even more, it was a time during which there were intense debates and disagreements about the appropriate methods for social research (for example, surveys versus qualitative case studies) (Whyte 1997, 98).

Whyte adapted to both disciplinary conflicts in ways that allowed him to assimilate and integrate the apparently contradictory views. He strove for the mastery level of adaptation rather than settling for embracing one view in a polar dichotomy and defensively rejecting the other. He said that at Harvard he "was conditioned to believe that if research was to be truly scientific, researchers' values must be set aside" (Whyte 1984, 19). Beginning with his experience in the Chicago sociology program, however, and continuing after that, Whyte increasingly found that he had to abandon the idea of a strict, mandatory separation between scientific research and action projects. In a statement indicating that he had begun working on the same bridge between science and social betterment that Mead envisioned, Whyte said he "began exploring how research can be integrated with action in ways that will advance science and enhance human progress at the same time" (1984, 20).

Whyte's approach to practicing sociology, in a way that promotes action change, has come to be termed *participatory action research* (PAR). In 1991, Whyte defined PAR as follows:

In participatory action research (PAR), some of the people in the organization or community under study participate actively with the professional researcher throughout the research process from the initial design to the final presentation of results and discussion of action implications. (Whyte 1991, 111)

In 1997, he added the following sentence to the definition "to bring in the *values* I see in PAR":

The social purpose underlying PAR is to empower low status people in the organization or community to make decisions and take actions which were previously foreclosed to them. (Whyte 1997, 112)

A well-known example of PAR took place after Xerox management proposed to outsource much of the work being done by union members, because of cost overruns. A consultant working with Whyte's guidance suggested to union and management leaders that they form a cost study team (CST). This CST would study ways to save money and jobs, thus harmonizing the perspectives and vested interests of both stakeholder groups. Even though there were perceived risks with this approach for both union and management, both sides agreed. With the consultant acting as facilitator, the CST worked creatively for six months and found ways of doing the work less expensively at Xerox than through outsourcing. Ultimately, 180 jobs and $3.2 million were saved.

Two important aspects of Whyte's approach to promoting action change within the PAR format should be noted. The first is that he does not see PAR as a method of promoting action change through "intervention." Rather, it is a way of facilitating problem-responsive action through creation, identification, and/or dissemination of social inventions. *Social inventions* are defined as:

- a new element in organizational structure or interorganizational relations;
- new sets of procedures for shaping human interactions and activities and the relations of humans to the natural and social environment;
- a new policy in action (that is, not just on paper); or
- a new role or set of roles. (Whyte 1997, 84)

Interventions cause change through imposition from outside the members' social world. Social inventions promote motivated change: actions change because members of social worlds can *see* that the changes allow effective resolution of their own problematic situations—problems with which they have been grappling.

The fact that the participatory research process is conducive to creation, identification, and/or dissemination of social inventions is an important reason why, as noted earlier, the social psychological dynamics of the situation in this approach promote buy-in to changed actions. A clear example of an instance in which Whyte's use of this type of approach facilitated problem-responsive action through identification and dissemination of a social invention is his work in the restaurant industry in the late 1940s (Whyte 1997, 58–59).

A chronic problem was friction between female waitpersons and male cooks. The male cooks would express their frustration at having to take orders from waitresses by stepping back from the counter, which left the waitresses waiting and fuming. A solution invented to respond to the observed friction problem was the "spindle," a spike that was installed on the serving counter in one test restaurant. Waitresses put their orders on the spike rather than giving them to the cooks. Friction was thus minimized through technology, because use of the spindle reduced the amount of interpersonal contact involved in status inferiors giving orders to status superiors. After the discovery of the spindle invention by Whyte's assistant, Edith Lentz, it became widely adopted in the restaurant industry.

The second important aspect of Whyte's PAR version of the problem-solving partnership approach to practicing sociology is that it focuses on promoting change in actions that occur within *sociotechnical systems*. Whyte said that he has come to see, based on his extensive work as a practicing sociologist in work organizations, that "the factory (or any work organization) is not only a social system but also a technical system, consisting of the technologies and tools and work procedures required to reach the organization's objectives" (Whyte 1997, 57). This is a point with enormous implications for the practicing sociologist: because the two systems are interdependent, "a change in the technical system necessarily impacts on the functioning of the social system, and a change in the social system has impacts on the technical system" (57). Thus, in the example, the invention of the spindle (part of the technological system) reduced friction between female waitpersons and male cooks (part of the social system).

Promotion of action change cannot occur in a vacuum. The sociocognitive framework that gives action meaning, and within which action occurs, must also be attended to by the practicing sociologist. This collectively generated cognitive framework, which gives coherence and direction to action, was called the "definition of the situation" by W. I. Thomas (Thomas and

Znaniecki 1918–1920, 73). The "definition of the situation" is really a collectively shared mental process of defining the situation, which exists in constant dynamic interplay with the collectively shared, overt process of act-construction (Blumer 1969). Social actors are in an ongoing, dynamic process of defining and redefining, to themselves and others, "what is going on here" and of constructing and reconstructing actions toward each other that correspond to the definitions.

Even though there is a dynamic, back-and-forth, interplay between defining and acting in the social contexts of real life, Thomas suggested that defining is logically prior to acting. The "Thomas theorem" says that situations defined as real will have real consequences because people act upon their definitions of what is "really" going on in the situation. Thomas used as an example the man who repeatedly attacked strangers on the street because his definition of the situation was that they were muttering vile things about him. Thomas thus implied that it behooves practicing sociologists to separate the strategies they direct at changing definitions of situations from those devoted to changing actions. Thomas was further saying that attending to changing definitions of situations may be more important for practicing sociologists than attempting to modify actions. At a minimum, he was saying that it is logical to try to modify the definitions of a situation before attempting to modify actions.

Roger Straus (1984) has proposed that the field of sociological practice focus its efforts exclusively on developing strategies for changing definitions of situations. Although I do not agree that this should be an exclusive focus for the field, I recognize that Straus has made an important initial contribution to organizing efforts in this area. Freely interpreted, Straus appears to be saying that there are four "levels" of social actors, ranging from more microlevel to more macro-level actors: persons, groups (including families and other informal groups), organizations (including structured social systems such as corporations, associations, communities, and governments), and social worlds (larger defined social wholes such as "the academic world" or the "sports world"). Persons interact within groups, organizations, and social worlds, and these latter, larger entities may be considered actors and interactors in their own right. Families, organizations, and social worlds also act and interact. Straus proposed strategies that can be used by practicing sociologists to change the definitions of situations and thus guide the actions and interactions of these varying levels of actors. He proposed direct, indirect, and cooperative approaches, all of which are focused on encouraging redefinition of "who we are" and "what is happening here."

Straus's various strategies for changing the definition of a situation may be seen as dedicated to resolution of a general (*definitional*) social problem which is logically prior to the various specific (*action*) problems confronting society today. These strategies promote the capacity of social actors at the various levels to act collectively toward resolution of whatever specific problems they are confronted with.

Lack of the capacity or readiness to act collectively is the master definitional problem with which we are confronted in our postmodern era. It may be termed a "community problem" (cf. Bellah et al. 1996; Etzioni 1988). Communal—which is to say mutually affirming and cooperative—social bonds are too much in a state of disrepair or rupture. Both within and among the groups, organizations, and social worlds in which we participate, we define ourselves too much as isolated and externally controlled.

We see ourselves as engaged in win-lose struggles against one another for infrequent opportunities for scarce material resources and social advancement. The specific action problems recognized in contemporary society (such as substance abuse, family violence, gang-related violent crime, poverty, racism, and war) can be seen as developing subsequent to, and partially as a consequence of, this definitional community problem. They represent defensive adaptational responses to situations in which actors at these varying levels of social action define themselves as "disconnected," "disempowered," "degraded," or "losing."

As practicing sociologists, then, a first order of business is the promotion of collaborative, communal definitions of situations among the social actors with whom we work. Such definitions of the situation promote readiness to act in ways that effectively respond to the myriad specific action problems confronting them. Depending on the level of social interaction where we work, our efforts in this regard should be dedicated to promoting social bonds both within and among groups.

We should be sensitized to the various dimensions and aspects of promoting socially bonded definitions of the situation by findings and principles from both sociological and psychological social psychology (Stephan and Stephan 1990; Cook, Fine, and House 1995). Especially helpful are principles derived from learning theory regarding promotion of learning relationships through modeling (see Bronfenbrenner 1970). Also important to recognize is the significance of activities in which people are mutually deferential (Scheff 1990) and in which there are "win-win" or "integrative" exchange relations (see Cook, Fine and House 1995, pt. II). Finally, it is critical to recognize that people define themselves as bonded with one another (and therefore ready to act to solve problems) when they can interpret their situations as "communal" within their own cultural traditions (see Hewitt 1988).

A basic social invention in the participatory inquiry approach to practicing sociology, for promoting collaborative definitions of situations as well as problem-responsive actions, is insider/outsider (I/O) research teams. I believe use of such teams will also help insulate practicing sociologists from the more punishing and marginalizing sociopolitical dynamics of their work situations. These teams were essentially envisioned by the Hull House sociologists and by Mead as integral to the "working hypothesis" process, and by Whyte and his colleagues when they formed the CST at Xerox. However, I/O teams were named and analyzed by organizational development researchers Bartunek and Louis (1996).

The basic idea is that forming bonds of partnership between researchers and practitioners in insider/outsider research teams can promote both a collaborative definition of the situation and action readiness among all the stakeholder groups represented on a team. Bartunek and Louis note that both the sociologist and the actor hold perspectives that are "situated," that is, ethnocentric or biased. Both perspectives are needed for effective problem solving. Bringing both of these perspectives together is clearly the goal of a partnership approach to practicing sociology. As noted, though, there are also sociopolitical dynamics in the working situation of practicing sociologists that make this difficult to accomplish, especially all at once and without guidance. Based on their review of the issues from the literature, as well as on their own study of "the faculty development committee," Bartunek and Louis identified stages in the development of I/O research teams that practicing sociologists can follow in a step-by-step fashion to overcome these difficulties (Bartunek and Louis 1996).

Bartunek and Louis concluded that the most important yield of I/O research teams is a kind of positive marginality. This positive marginality contrasts with the punishing double marginality sometimes encountered by practicing sociologists who operate outside the context of an I/O team (as in the experience of Rossi, described earlier). This positive marginality is based on mutual interdependence and mutual respect that promote effective problem solving. Bartunek and Louis wrote: "In insider/outsider pairings, the outsider's assumptions, language and cognitive frames are made explicit in the insider's questions and vice-versa. The parties, in a colloquial sense, keep each other honest—or at least more conscious than a single party alone may easily achieve" (1996, 62).

Concluding, Bartunek and Louis made three points about the positive marginality experienced by members of I/O teams. First, it is based on maintaining both *distance* and *relationship*. Second, it is also based on power equality. Outside researchers are not seen as sole possessors and controllers of legitimate interpretations of the situation. Nor are practitioners so viewed. Finally, increased empowerment is experienced by both the insider and the outsider members of the partnership. For our purposes, Bartunek and Louis emphasized that use of the power of sociology is not likely to be effective unless practicing sociologists establish relationships of power equality with the users of that knowledge.

A SOCIOLOGICAL PRACTICE JOURNEY

On March 24, 1989, the supertanker *Exxon Valdez* ran aground on Bligh Reef in Prince William Sound (PWS), Alaska, releasing 42 million liters of oil into local waters. It was the largest oil spill in U.S. history. The oil spill (EVOS) covered more than 3,000 square miles of water and affected more than 1,200 miles of shoreline. The accident led to the death of about 350,000 birds; between 3,500 and 5,500 sea otters; 30 harbor seals; 17 gray whales; and 14 sea lions. As one Native Alaskan leader said, the day EVOS occurred was "the day the water died" (Picou et al. 1992).

By August 19, 1989, University of South Alabama sociology professor J. Steven Picou and his colleagues were in Cordova, Alaska. Originally, their project was not intended to contain a major sociological practice component. The project was envisioned as basic research on the long-term social impacts of the spill on the rural communities of PWS. The populations of those communities include high numbers of "subsistence economy" Native Alaskans and commercial fishermen. The lives of both groups are sustained by traditional subsistence activities that depend on the water in PWS being "alive." What Steve Picou did not anticipate at the time was that his project would continue for a decade and would evolve into a highly instructive sociological practice episode, in terms of many of the features discussed throughout this chapter. Picou and his colleagues were faced with, and innovatively and effectively responded to, many of the challenges of the collaborative inquiry approach to sociological practice.

The focus of their project became stress. They documented long-term, chronic stress in the affected communities, and as time went on they effectively established strong insider/outsider bonds with many members of those communities. As their bonds of trust with the communities grew stronger, they worked collaboratively with these rural communities to organize a program to assist in the recovery from the EVOS-induced stress.

Along the way, Steve Picou himself experienced high levels of professional and personal stress, to which he also responded effectively. His own stress was caused by the kind of sociopolitical dynamics that lead to experiences of marginalization, as discussed earlier. Specifically, he was the subject of litigation through which Exxon attempted to gain access to his raw data and other information, in ways that threatened to breach the confidentiality he had promised his informants. Exxon claimed it needed this information because Picou's findings about levels of community stress from the spill were being cited by experts speaking on behalf of 3,000 individuals who had filed damage suits against Exxon (Marshall 1993). Also in the context of that litigation, stress was created for Picou by criticism of his work in court by two sociologists who were hired as expert witnesses for Exxon. Ironically, the sociologists hired by Exxon and who attacked Picou's credibility included Peter Rossi, whose own story of stressful experience stemming from the sociopolitical context of his applied work was discussed earlier in this chapter (Lodwick 1994).

When Steve Picou was in the sociology graduate program at Louisiana State University in Baton Rouge in 1969, he read Becker's "Whose Side Are We On?" and was exposed to Herbert Blumer's (1969) version of the symbolic interactionist perspective on which Becker's article is based. The major transmitter of these ideas at the time at LSU was professor Vernon Parenton. Parenton, a rural South Louisiana native who attended Harvard on a General Education Board fellowship and was named an Austin Fellow, received his Ph.D. in sociology under Pitrim Sorokin. From Sorokin, Parenton inherited the view that *culture* consists of a system of meanings that anchors the selves of members of the group and therefore gives coherence to the social interactions of the members (Sorokin 1962, ch. 3).

At LSU, Parenton sought to blend the sociocultural system perspective of

Sorokin with the pragmatist approach of the Chicago School, especially as represented in Blumer's work. Parenton impressed on Picou and his other students the importance of studying local communities and other local groups as interacting individuals. Parenton urged students to work from the idea that locality groups actively and innovatively construct and use symbolic culture as shared tools to give identity-supporting meaning to their collective problematic situations and to interactively construct a course of action.

Steve Picou used the sociocultural, interactionist perspective, in which he had been steeped at LSU, in his teaching about and in his research on technological disasters over the years. In doing so, he followed the dictum of Ogburn (cited earlier), which was taught in the LSU sociology program and in most other sociology programs. He treated the sociology he had learned as a science only, and, as such, not concerned directly with making the world a better place. Rather, he used the sociocultural, interactionist perspective he was taught at LSU only to generate and disseminate knowledge, as an outside observer, about individuals interacting as members of impacted communities. It was not until his involvement in the PWS project that he considered applying these notions in a reflexive way, to create a problem-solving relationship between him and the community being studied.

Steve Picou's ability and inclination to apply his sociocultural, interactionist perspective to promote problem-responsive change in PWS grew in proportion to the growth of an I/O relationship between him as a sociologist and the PWS community. As he became close to the community, he increasingly realized that his research and educational activities were having an unanticipated effect on community people, an effect that could be interpreted in light of interactionist theory. For example, he tells the following story. On a visit to the same fishing village on PWS that he has been intensively studying for a number of years, he addressed a citizen's workshop on the aftermath of EVOS. In the course of his presentation he described the village as entering the recovery stage. Shortly after the workshop, as he stood on a street corner, he overheard the following conversation between two people, referred to as persons A and B:

A: What's going on at the lodge?
B: Dr. Picou's back in town making a presentation.
A: Well, did he ride in on his white horse to tell us about our problems?
B: He's talking about stages people go through after disaster.

A: Really. Well, what stage are we in?
B: Recovery.
A: Cool. That sounds good to me. (Picou 1996, cited in Kroll-Smith and Gunter 1997, 172)

Picou and his associates reflected on experiences like this, while conducting disaster research, in light of sociocultural interactionist theory. They concluded that such instances of researcher influence on the community illustrate the "reciprocal hermeneutic, or the idea that as we are interpreting them they are interpreting us" (Kroll-Smith and Gunter 1997, 173).

A second result of the strengthening bond between researchers and community members was that Picou and his associates became more and more sympathetic to the plight of the community. In terms of Becker's perspective (Becker 1967), discussed earlier, Picou and his associates were increasingly "taking sides" with the community. The chronic stress that their research showed EVOS had produced in the lives of community members became more and more of a concern to the sociologists.

Over time, Steve Picou and his colleagues became strongly disposed to organize a program, based on symbolic interactionist premises, designed to mitigate the community's chronic stress. In a word, they moved increasingly away from the traditional, generate-and-disseminate-new-knowledge approach to sociology, and increasingly toward a practicing sociology approach. An opportunity arose to practice sociology, using the participatory problem-solving approach, when the PWS Regional Citizen's Advisory Council (RCAC) agreed to sponsor them in organizing a participatory research-based program for community stress reduction. As a result, Steve and his colleagues worked collaboratively with the community in designing the "Growing Together Community Education Program," which was proven to reduce EVOS-related stress in the community.

CONCLUDING COMMENTS

The development of symbolic interactionist theory in its most recent phase has not been covered in this chapter. Jonathan H. Turner (1982) has summarized the major trends, and Ralph H. Turner (1979–1980) has written extensively on role theory and related aspects of this approach for more than a quarter of a century. Sheldon Stryker (1980) brought the theory up to date in work that has connected it with current advances in knowledge about the relation between personality and social structure. What I have focused upon is the potential of interactionism for sociological practice; Turner and Stryker have concerned themselves primarily with issues in the academic discipline itself.

There is, in fact, an enduring gap between practice and sociological theory. The interactionist approach has, as I have emphasized, offered excellent resources to practitioners. Functionalist, system, conflict, and critical theory have seldom been relied upon in practice to any extent. Likewise, just as practitioners do much of their work without explicit regard for theory, so academic theory builders rarely draw upon applied sociology to refine their propositions.

Helpful as interactionism has been for sixty years, it seldom guides or illuminates applied projects in which co-participation is not feasible. The democratic ideals of sharing, partnering, and close work between social scientist and client group or community are too precious to be treated lightly. When they can be pursued, their worth is enormous. Nevertheless, there are many, many instances—springing from courts, macro-social problems of enormous magnitude and potential for conflict, and other sources—when these ideals have been violated or discarded long before the sociologist reaches the setting.

Many sociological theories have been designed, understandably, in the service of the discipline. They focus almost wholly upon enabling the creation of knowledge for its own sake or for furtherance of the academic discipline, and are rarely of service for applications. As the discipline has become more fragmented into subspecialties in recent decades, moreover, theory has broken away from substantive portions of the field and is a matter of discourse primarily between theoreticians. Interactionism remains of great value to practitioners, especially in their work on sociotherapy, community organization, program planning for inducing social change and adaptation, and criminal justice reforms. It does not play much of a role in large-scale survey research, demography, data analysis in general, and socioeconomic development projects.

REFERENCES

Addams, J. 1895. *Hull-House Maps and Papers, by Residents of Hull-House, a Social Settlement. A Presentation of Nationalities and Wages in a Congested District of*

Chicago, Together with Comments and Essays on Problems Growing out of the Social Conditions. Boston: Crowell.

Anderson, N. 1923. *The Hobo.* Chicago: University of Chicago Press. [Reprint 1961.]

Argyris, C., R. Putnam, and D. McLain Smith. 1985. *Action Science.* San Francisco: Jossey-Bass.

Bartunek, J. M., and M. Louis. 1996. *Insider/Outsider Team Research.* Thousand Oaks, Calif.: Sage Publications.

Becker, E. 1971. *The Lost Science of Man.* New York: Braziller.

Becker, H. 1966. Introduction. In *The Jackroller: A Delinquent Boy's Own Story,* v–xviii. Chicago: University of Chicago Press.

———. 1967. Whose side are we on? *Social Problems* 14 (Winter): 239–47.

Bellah, R., R. Madsen, W. M. Sullivan, A. Swidler, and S. M. Tipton. 1996. *Habits of the Heart.* Berkeley: University of California Press.

Blumer, H. 1969. *Symbolic Interactionism.* Englewood Cliffs, N.J.: Prentice-Hall.

Bulmer, M. 1984. *The Chicago School of Sociology: Institutionalization, Diversity, and the Rise of Sociological Research.* Chicago: University of Chicago Press.

Bronfenbrenner, U. 1970. *Two Worlds of Childhood.* New York: Touchstone.

Cook, K. S., G. A. Fine, and J. S. House, eds. 1995. *Sociological Perspectives on Social Psychology.* Boston: Allyn & Bacon.

Coser, L. A. 1956. *The Functions of Social Conflict.* New York: Free Press.

Cousins, J. B. 1996. Consequences of researcher involvement in participatory evaluation. *Studies in Educational Evaluation* 22: 3–27.

Dahrendorf, R. 1959. *Class and Class Conflict in Industrial Society.* Stanford, Calif.: Stanford University Press.

Darling, R. B. 1996. Syllabus for "Methods for Sociological Practice." In *The Clinical Sociology Resource Book*, edited by J. M. Fritz. Washington, D.C.: ASA Teaching Resources Center.

Deegan, M. J. 1986. *Jane Addams and the Men of the Chicago School.* New Brunswick, N.J.: Transaction Books.

Dentler, R. A. August 1995. The linkage of theory and practice. Paper presented at the annual meeting of the American Sociological Association, Washington, D.C.

Denzin, N. K. 1989. *Interpretive Interactionism.* Newbury Park, Calif.: Sage Publications.

Deutscher, I., F. P. Pestello, and H. F. G. Pastel. 1993. *Sentiments and Acts.* Hawthorne, N.Y.: Aldine De Gruyter.

Etzioni, A. 1988. *The Moral Dimension: Toward a New Economics.* New York: Free Press.

Faris, R. E. L. 1967. *Chicago Sociology, 1920–1932.* Chicago: University of Chicago Press.

Fisher, R. J. 1982. *Social Psychology: An Applied Approach.* New York: St. Martin's Press.

Fitzgerald, E. 1990. *Endless Crusade: Women Social Scientists and Progressive Reform.* New York: Oxford University Press.

Glaser, B. G., and A. L. Strauss. 1967. *The Discovery of Grounded Theory*. Chicago: Aldine De Gruyter.

Golan, N. 1981. *Passing Through Transitions: A Guide for Practitioners*. New York: Free Press.

Hewitt, J. P. 1988. *Self and Society: A Symbolic Interactionist Social Psychology*. Boston: Allyn & Bacon.

Hughes, E. C. 1949. Social change and status protest. *Phylon* 10 (First Quarter): 58–65.

Iutcovich, J. M., and M. Iutcovich. 1987. *The Sociologist as Consultant*. New York: Praeger.

Kroll-Smith, S., and V. J. Gunter. 1997. Legislators, interpreters, and disasters. In *Theories of Disaster*, edited by E. L. Quarantelli. London: Routledge.

Lewin, K. 1946. Action research and minority problems. *Journal of Social Issues* 2: 34–46.

Lodwick, D. G. 1994. Attacks on sociological research. *Useful Sociologist* 16: 3, 13.

Marshall, E. 1993. Court orders "sharing" of data. *Science* 261: 284–86.

Matthews, F. 1977. *Quest for an American Sociology: Robert E. Park and the Chicago School*. Montreal: McGill University Press.

Merton, R. K. 1957. *Social Theory and Social Structure*. New York: Free Press.

Merton, R. K. 1967. *On Theoretical Sociology*. New York: Free Press.

Parsons, T. 1960. *Structure and Process in Modern Societies*. New York: Free Press.

———. 1949. *The Structure of Social Action*. Glencoe, Ill.: Free Press.

Pettigrew, T. F., ed. 1980. *The Sociology of Race Relations*. New York: Free Press.

Picou, J. S., D. A. Gill, C. L. Dyer, and E. W. Curry. 1992. Disruption and stress in an Alaskan fishing community: Initial and continuing impacts of the *Exxon Valdez* oil spill. *Industrial Crisis Quarterly* 6: 235–57.

Picou, J. S. 1996. Compelled disclosure of scholarly research: Some comments on "high stakes litigation." *Law and Contemporary Problems* 59, no. 3: 149–58. See also C. Parate et al. 2000. Coping with technological disaster. *Journal of Traumatic Stress* 13 (pt. 1): 23–40.

Rauschenbush, W. 1979. *Robert E. Park: Biography of a Sociologist*. Durham, N.C.: Duke University Press.

Ritzer, G. 1993. *Sociological Beginnings: On the Origins of Key Ideas in Sociology*. New York: McGraw-Hill.

Rossi, P. 1987. No good applied social research goes unpunished. *Society* 25 (November/December): 74–79.

Scheff, T. J. 1990. *Microsociology: Discourse, Emotion, and Social Structure*. Chicago: University of Chicago Press.

Shaw, C. R. 1931. *The Natural History of a Delinquent Career*. Chicago: University of Chicago Press.

Simmons, O. E. 1994. Grounded therapy. In *More Grounded Theory Methodology: A Reader*, edited by Barney G. Glaser, 4–37. Mill Valley, Calif.: Sociology Press.

Smith, M. F. 1989. *Evaluability Assessment: A Practical Approach*. Boston: Kluwer Academic Publishers.

Sorokin, P. 1962. *Society, Culture, and Personality: Their Structure and Dynamics*. New York: Cooper Square.

Stephan, C. W., and W. G. Stephan. 1990. *Two Social Psychologies*. Belmont, Calif.: Wadsworth.

Stonequist, E. V. 1937. *The Marginal Man*. New York: Scribner's.

Straus, R. A. 1984. Changing the definition of the situation: Toward a theory of sociological intervention. *Clinical Sociology Review* 2: 51–63.

Stryker, S. 1980. *Symbolic Interactionism*. Menlo Park, Calif.: Benjamin Cummings.

Thomas, W. I., and F. Znaniecki. 1918–1920. *The Polish Peasant in Europe and America*. Boston: Gorham.

Turner, J. H. 1982. *The Structure of Sociological Theory*. Homewood, Ill.: Dorsey Press.

Turner, R. H. 1979–1980. Strategy for developing an integrated role theory. *Humboldt Journal of Social Relations* 7 (Fall-Winter): 123–39.

White, R. W. 1974. Strategies of adaptation: An attempt at systematic description." In *Coping and Adaptation*, edited by George V. Coehlo, David A. Hamburg, and John E. Adams, 47–68. New York: Basic Books.

Whyte, W. F. 1997. *Creative Problem Solving in the Field: Reflections on a Career*. Walnut Creek, Calif.: Altamira Press.

———. 1984. *Learning from the Field: A Guide from Experience*. Beverly Hills, Calif.: Sage Publications.

———, ed. 1991. *Participatory Action Research*. Newbury Park, Calif.: Sage Publications.

3

Organizations

INTRODUCTION

Sociologists have practiced in a wide range of complex, formal organizations, including business and industry, government, hospitals, the military, and religious and other voluntary associations, ever since the 1930s. This chapter reviews some of their activities and achievements and synthesizes the distinctive and continuing relation between sociological practice and organizations.

HISTORY

Until a century and a half ago, social life throughout the cultures of the world took place mainly within primary groups and similarly informal settings: the family, cottage industries, religious congregations, and rural communities. In contrast, today's social landscape in the developed economies is dominated by large, complex organizations. We are usually born in hospitals, cared for by day in children's centers, schooled in classrooms controlled by functionaries of the state, enrolled in formally structured universities, and put to work in corporations. Some of the organizations we inhabit are voluntary; some are obligatory, such as schools and prisons; and others are utilitarian, but all tend to be formal organizations that are intentionally and rationally designed to achieve certain objectives.

In the thinking of the seminal sociologists of the second half of the nineteenth century—Herbert Spencer, Karl Marx, Emile Durkheim, and, above
all, Max Weber—the evolutionary processes determining this vast change in
social organization were social differentiation, incremental divisions of labor,
economic production, and rationalization. At the very core of the emergence
of complex, formal organizations in most institutional domains is a process
of rationalization in which customs, fairly spontaneous traditions, and myths
and legends are supplanted or become bound up by abstract, explicit, and
consciously devised rules and procedures. Friendships, interpersonal attachments and power conflicts, love relations, and sexuality are among the few
remaining primary units of human transaction. One of the most common
products of rationalization is, of course, a *bureaucracy*, key features of which
are a hierarchy of authority statuses, a formalized mode of organization, and
a set of operating rules that govern exchanges and outcomes.

Factories came into being in all Western economies at the beginning of the
nineteenth century. They expressed in full detail the characteristics of bureau-
cratic organizations: each operation was separated from the others as part of
an overall plan; workers were stratified so that those on the bottom had the
narrowest span of control over each part of their work and those on the top
had the broadest; the parts of the plan were coordinated through an administration; each activity was scheduled; and human relations were separated from
the formal properties of the positions within the structure. As with military
systems, in which seamen on board a battleship are defined as personnel features of a weapons system, people were attached to the tools, the hardware,
and the physical products of the factory.

The factory as an organization had such enormous production efficacy,
especially as steam power came to be available, that the model expanded culturally to become a kind of guiding paradigm for other institutions. By the
end of the century, for example, public schools had been redesigned to operate as factories, and their architecture reflected this change.

In the era of the steam-powered, stand-alone factory (1850–1910), social
scientists were seldom engaged in organizational studies. Their concerns in
this period were with larger institutional trends, such as capitalism and the
nature of social change at the macro level. Just as the factory itself was a product of the application of science, however, so the organization of factory work
first came under would-be scientific scrutiny at the hands of Frederick W.
Taylor, a machinist in a steel plant who became a mechanical engineer in

1893. The American Society of Mechanical Engineers, founded in 1880, was becoming the godfather of "management engineering," and this interest among its members led to the formation of the Society for the Promotion of the Science of Management in 1912.

Taylor, as a young gang boss in a steel plant, dedicated himself to measuring what ought to constitute a "fair day's work," as he called it, as he observed that workers regularly held back the rate of production through group cooperation. He began to experiment with ways to speed up labor. He studied worker fatigue, methods of shoveling, inspection operations, pig-iron handling, and metal cutting. Accurate time study of every motion entailed in factory labor became his method, which came to be known as Taylorism and which shapes production methods in many factories and offices to this day (Taylor 1911). Taylor at first believed that workers would gladly accept new methods when they learned that increased efficiency could result in higher wages. He also thought that workers with relatively low production rates would earn such low wages as to cause them to choose between upgrading their labor or quitting, thus generating a kind of Darwinian improvement of the quality of the work force. Within a few years, Taylor realized that nearly all workers hated his interventions and regarded them as intrusive, alienating coercions by management. Years later, the more powerful unions formed during the 1940s began to condemn time study practices and to resist their use. As the leaders of the United Auto Workers asked its members, "Whose time does the stopwatch keep?"

Industrial psychology came to life in the same era as Taylorism. The quest for measures of individual differences undertaken by James McKeen Cattell at Columbia University, at the close of the nineteenth century, fused with the Darwinian ideology of the quest for the fittest candidates for the work force. Henry C. Link wrote, "The ideal employment method is undoubtedly an immense machine which would receive applicants of all kinds at one end, automatically sort, interview, and record them, and finally turn them out at the other end nicely labeled with the job to which they are to go" (1918, 184–85). Systematic psychology thus became joined at the hip with personnel management and matured into personnel psychology in the service of management.

With the rapid rise of regionally dispersed production facilities, the growth of national corporations, the evolution of mass markets, and the new technologies of electrical power, wireless communications, and the automobile and airplane, sociologists began to change their focus. One powerful impetus behind projects in industrial sociology was unionism and the rise of conflicts within the ranks of factory workers. Many college students and professors in the 1920s combined studies in sociology with studies in economics, and some undertook field research in industrial work settings. E. T. Hiller edited a book of studies and analytic essays entitled *The Strike* (1928), for example.

From its inception, sociological practice in what came to be known as organization development (OD) on the one hand, and industrial sociology on the other, tended to apply its science to the situation of workers, first inside factories, then in their emerging unions, and then inside office occupations and professions. With its roots in Karl Marx's idea of the alienation of workers, Emile Durkheim's emphasis on anomie, Max Weber's conceptualization of bureaucracy, and Lester Ward's search for a positive evolution toward human betterment, this focus was to be expected. I discuss parts of this tradition in chapter 4 on labor relations.

CONTEMPORARY PATTERNS OF PRACTICE

Spurred intensely by the urgencies of World War II, sociologists, in close association with psychologists and management specialists, began to concentrate on problems of formal organization itself as a source of quality and speed of work activities of all kinds. A good example of this focus came in the work of sociological practitioner Elton Mayo and his industrial research staff at Harvard University. He was asked by the government to study the problem of aircraft turnover in the aircraft industry in southern California in 1943, at the height of the war, when labor turnover in plants just one or two years earlier reached 70 to 80 percent.

Mayo's team found that the group sentiments and informal teaming of workers in the aircraft plants were constantly being ripped apart by the demands of management for loans and transfers of workers. The workers' basic need to form small groups in which loyalty and trustworthy social interaction could evolve was being undermined by change imposed from above and by the production requirements of the external situation. Of his team's efforts to intervene by devising ways of building the spontaneous cooperation of employees, Mayo wrote that he

had not fully realized in 1932 . . . how profoundly the social structure of civilization has been shaken by scientific, engineering, and industrial development. . . . The management problem appears at its acutest in the work of the supervisor. No longer does the supervisor work with a team of persons that he has known for many years or perhaps a lifetime; he is a leader of a group of individuals that forms and disappears almost as he watches it. (Mayo 1944, 75)

Mayo's group applied the earlier social theory of Charles H. Cooley (1909) to the work situations of the aircraft factories: the challenge for contemporary society, said Cooley, was how to build primary group life. Mayo found that well-knit teams of workers were the ones that created quasi-primary groups while working together on the plant floor, where positive group morale reduced absenteeism and increased productivity as byproducts of group cohesion and loyalty. The general proposition, still central to organization development to this day, was that workers' need for social recognition and an interpersonal sense of belonging is more crucial to morale—and hence performance—than any of the physical or mechanical conditions within the work setting.

Sociologists were instrumental, then, in developing a conceptual alternative to the very foundation of the organization of work from the factory to the post-factory era. Douglas McGregor, in *The Human Side of Enterprise* (1960), summarized the alternatives as Theories X and Y. Under X, we assume that most people do not like the work they do and will avoid it if they can. Given this disposition, most people must be coerced, directed, and frightened by threats of sanctions if they are to put out an adequate work effort. What is more, most people prefer to be directed, seek to avoid taking responsibility, and have little ambition. Under Y, in contrast, we assume that working is, for most people, as natural an activity as play; that people like to exercise autonomy, variety, and self-direction in the course of their work; and that people prefer to group together in their work to share common objectives and to reinforce one another.

Theory Y enthusiasts include most practicing sociologists. They organized with psychologists, behavioral organization specialists, and human resource specialists into the American Society for Training and Development in 1944. Today, this association has 70,000 members who come from more than 150 countries around the globe. They work not only in business and industry but also in federal and state government agencies and in colleges and universities. Their main periodical, *Training and Development*, is one of the world's leading sources of applied knowledge about organizational analysis and change.

THE TAVISTOCK INSTITUTE

The Tavistock Clinic was set up in England in 1920 to research and develop treatments for a range of "neurotic disabilities," such as "shell shock," encountered in World War I (Trist and Murray 1990). In the late 1930s, clinic staffers, nearly all of whom had with medical training, began to move away from a psychotherapeutic focus on neurotic disabilities toward a more general exploration of human resource problems facing the British Army. Immediately after World War II, the Clinic began to help in designing and advocating for the National Health Service in the United Kingdom, while its staff's initial focus widened further to include a variety of social problems that went beyond mental health. Its 1946 reestablishment as the Tavistock Institute was first funded by a large grant from the Rockefeller Foundation.

Formed by the confluence of two wars, military needs, and the medical model of treatment, the Tavistock Institute became, in the first ten years of its formation, a world-class center that gathered in clinical psychologists, psychoanalysts, social psychologists, and sociologists. Its strategic focus became an innovative form of sociological practice, transforming industries and businesses through what it called *action research* in organizational redesign and change. As Joe Cullen, Dean of Scientific Affairs at Tavistock wrote, this pioneering effort implied

a commitment to the democratization of social relations, and indeed the sociotechnical approach applied in the early days of the Institute to work re-engineering and organizational change . . . resonates with notions of empowerment and subject engagement in action. . . . The Tavistock action research manifesto presents itself almost as a higher plane of social science, building bridges between the "scientific" and the "sociological" imagination; engaging people as co-participants in research endeavor, rather than as subjects to be scrutinized; committing itself to societal transformation through social engagement. (Cullen 1998, 1544)

Tavistock practitioners researched the structural and social interactive sources of worker morale, productivity, and performance quality, and devised techniques of sensitivity training, team building, and co-participative involvement of employees in corporate decision making. As organizational development (OD) evolved as a profession within firms as part of personnel offices (today restyled as human resource divisions or units), and as organizational behavior came to be built into the standard curriculum of business management degree programs, it was the cluster of ideas, intervention experiments, and reports from the Tavistock Institute that became the foundation of the emerging field.

Tavistock's American "collaborators" included many social psychologists, some of them trained in sociology, who pioneered in the engineering of team building in the 1940s and 1950s. Initially, these practitioners created T groups (T for training) as small group experiments in group dynamics. The first groups were composed of collections of strangers, often undergraduates, and the practitioners would observe how a structure of norms and sentiments evolved spontaneously. Later T group applications, used to this day in conferencing and training programs, fitted their approach to already-formed employee teams and to voluntary-association communities of members in churches, clubs, and social agencies. Goal setting, decision making, role clarification, and organizational change projects are among the most universal T group activities of the current era (Dyer 1994).

THE CLINICAL APPROACH

Just as Tavistock began as a clinic in medical psychology, so the Menninger Clinic and Foundation in Kansas (recently relocated to Texas) pioneered in the use of psychoanalytic theory in conceptualizing, diagnosing, and treating mental health issues in the organizational workplace. The Menninger leader was Harry Levinson. His work, begun in 1955, was concerned with the problems of the individual at work. His early focus was on accidents in the workplace, absenteeism, and alcoholism. As the work of his group evolved, Levinson and his associates became convinced that the organizational context and climate surrounding employees often played a major role in the generation or resolution of their mental health challenges.

In the psychotherapeutic tradition, Levinson's approach was diagnostic. He offered opportunities for corporate leaders to allow his teams into their workplaces to carry out studies as consultants, knowing full well that scrutiny, measurement, and analysis were in themselves not only a consultative action but an intervention as well, as the workplace participants came to be involved in self-reflection, interpretations of contexts, and proactive in seeking information and guidance on how to improve their organizations. Levinson's methods and techniques were, with few exceptions, those of field sociology: attitude surveys, demographic analyses, focus group interviews, and field observation. Meticulous case studies resulted, along with prognostic recommendations for improving the context and the climate of the workplace (Levinson 1972).

Levinson's approach has attracted the interest of some clinical sociologists. John G. Bruhn, in "The Organization as a Person," wrote:

Clinical sociologists are often asked to be consultants to organizations, usually when they are in trouble, and usually from the perspective of the total organization, its subsystems, or groups. Sociologists are not inclined to focus on either individuals or the characteristics attributed to individuals. However . . . the author suggests that the process of diagnosis, treatment, and rehabilitation of organizations could be strengthened if some analogies appropriate to persons are used in consulting with organizations. (Bruhn 1997, 53)

Sociological positivists of the nineteenth century were fond of analyzing societies through the prism of the individual biological organism, an analogy that was discredited decades later as knowledge about societies and about organisms increased; yet Bruhn and many clinical sociologists today make a quite direct analogy between individual personality and complex organizations. Bruhn argues that organizations, like egos, have boundaries. Schaef and Fassel state their conviction that "organizations that have become addicted to their paradigms no longer are responsive to the needs of the clients they propose to serve" (1988). Organizations have life cycles, self-concepts, unique life histories and languages, and a health status. Kets de Vries and Miller (1991) think of "dysfunctional" organizations in the terms of abnormal psychology: there are paranoid organizations, depressive organizations, and schizoid organizations. Bruhn writes, "Sick organizations, like sick individuals, may not perceive themselves as needing help. . . . Intervention in sick organizations, when invited, usually needs to be preceded by a thorough 'history and physical' to decide whether the illness is acute or chronic and its prognosis, with or without intervention" (Bruhn 1997, 61).

The difference between Levinson's Menninger Clinic approach and the approach of Bruhn and other clinical sociologists is negligible at one level of interpretation. Both adopt psychomedical models developed by clinical medicine and apply them to the scrutinized condition of an organization. Both diagnose and aspire to treat the patient. Levinson, however, focuses on the mental health of employees, so that his approach takes the organization as an environment but remains centered on the individuals who inhabit it. Bruhn focuses on the organization itself as a patient.

Delbert C. Miller and William H. Form, in their treatise, *Industrial Sociology: Work in Organizational Life*, do not share the clinical perspective. They assert that

[o]ne of the most fundamental ideas [of sociologists] is that people can be understood only in their social relations with one another. *Social relations, not individuals, are the basic units of observation.* Since social relations constitute the essence of groups, sociologists begin looking for social relations or groups whenever they examine human activity. . . .

The sociological point of view does not demand an examination of the relations of specific individuals and situations. Rather, it seeks to find the kinds of social relations that may be expected to develop under certain stable conditions. (Miller and Form 1980, 285)

Their perspective and that of Bruhn and other clinical sociologists of the 1990s are not irreconcilable. What is more, OD consultants enter their clients' organizations as a team whose members often come from several fields and professions; the sociological perspective is represented but seldom dominant or unilateral in its application. In fact, OD leadership is most often in the hands of business managers trained by management schools in behavioral organization, which is a professional blend of human resource management theories, applied psychology, sociology, and a host of other domains.

A renowned champion of the merged disciplinary approach to corporate organizations is sociologist Rosabeth Moss Kanter. She had authored or edited seven books and many articles on corporate development questions before she wrote her initially most famous work, *The Change Masters: Innovation for Productivity in the American Corporation* (1983). Her thesis was that American corporations could revive their comparatively flagging productivity by fostering internal innovation. The vision is fundamentally a gospel of hope for democratically stimulated change, invention, and adaptation to external forces such as globalization:

People at all levels, including ordinary people at the grass roots and middle managers at the head[s] of department, can contribute to solving organizational problems, to inventing new methods or pieces of strategies. . . . These "corporate entrepreneurs" can help their organizations to experiment on uncharted territories and to move beyond what is known into the realm of innovation—if the power to do this is available, and if the organization knows how to take advantage of their enterprise. Those "ifs" are the subject of this book. (Kanter 1983, 23)

Kanter writes that she spent five years preparing the ideas and findings of *The Change Masters*, visiting, observing, and interviewing with assistants, hundreds of officials, and employees of more than fifty American corporations. The book's appendices outline her sociological methods and techniques for doing her field studies. Her ability to glean explanatory clues from her own field observations and those of her research teammates is exceptionally strong and well communicated, but her conceptual framework and her conclusions alike are grounded in organizational sociology and social psychology. They go back to the group foundations of thought about work and corporate structures:

The highest proportion of entrepreneurial accomplishment is found in the companies that are least segmented and segmentalist, companies that instead have integrative structures and cultures emphasizing pride, commitment, collaboration, and teamwork. . . . Companies producing more managerial entrepreneurs . . . [have managers who] are encouraged to take initiative and to behave cooperatively. (Kanter 1983, 178)

Kanter's comparative method consistently contrasts traditional with innovative corporations. Her data collection, analyses, and interpretations include not only senior executives and middle managers, but also the line and staff workers at the base of the large companies in her sample. Kanter concluded her book, and those that followed *The Change Masters*, with recipes for becoming flexibly adaptive and innovative, and she consults frequently with interested leaders on how to begin the transformative process.

Her prescriptions include many ideas that hark back as far as the work of Elton Mayo: increase employee participation and involvement; build a sense of primary community within the corporation; create an integrative structure that maintains the regular units devoted to conducting routine business with units that interlock with them yet are devoted to entrepreneurial innovation. Her focus is consistently fixed on social relations between groups of employees and executives and on the relations between groups, but she does not endorse the Japanese approach to committees and groups in which individuals are subordinated to groups in the decision process: "American-style participation does not mean the dominance of committees over individuals, the submergence of the individual in the group, or the swallowing of the person by the team, but rather *the mechanism for giving more people at more levels a piece of the entrepreneurial action*" (364).

Kanter thus does not make innovations in sociological practice in her work;

she does, however, merge happily with trends in the business management field of behavioral organization. In this way her emphasis remains upon corporate productivity, as distinguished from employee morale, mental health, or organizational analysis for its own sake. Her methods are the traditional ones of applied social research and her conclusions closely parallel those of Tom Peters and other eminent business writers who celebrate forms of corporate transformation and reorganization within corporate America.

EMPOWERMENT

Spurred in part by the work of Rosabeth Kanter, the OD community's use of the idea of employee empowerment became frequent and very popular with corporations and nonprofit organizations during the 1990s. The idea, remember, involves reorganizing work statuses, roles, and training in ways that increase the ability of workforce groups and individuals to make more autonomous decisions and to participate more vigorously in the power structure of their companies and agencies. A survey of Fortune 1000 companies found that 47 percent of these firms had instituted some form of empowered work teams with at least some of their workers, and 60 percent planned to increase their employee involvement over the next two years (Lawler, Mohrman, and Ledford 1992). Leaders in these companies and OD enthusiasts believe that empowerment increases product quality and customer service by driving decision-making authority down to those workers closest to the product or the customer, but also inculcates a sense of job ownership, commitment, and efficacy while increasing net profitability.

Robin D. Johnson and Elizabeth K. Thurston (1997) have summarized some of the ways in which the empowerment strategy can be implemented, based on field practice trials:

1. Real groups of employees who interdepend on one another (as distinguished from co-acting groups of those who do the same tasks and report to a common supervisor) should be reinforced and multiplied.. The domain of real groups whose members are measured and rewarded as groups should be enlarged; their members should be linked within groups to larger teams comprising a number of such groups. Competitive performances of individuals do not help develop real groups; trust and cohesiveness within groups and teams are the key.

2. Diversity of gender, race, ethnicity, and age is a source of new ideas and corrective contributions. Thus, diverse teams offer substantially greater creativity and precision; however, they are harder to build and sustain.

3. "Administrative theorists, social scientists, consultants, and practitioners have all
   created a number of definitions which vary across the . . . dimensions of power,
   authority, control, responsibility, efficacy, interdependence, task motivation, commitment, deviance, support, and trust. . . . With so many possible variations on
   empowerment, no wonder only 10 percent of Fortune 1000 employees feel empowered." (Johnson and Thurston 1997, 68)

TOTAL QUALITY MANAGEMENT

OD professionals in the 1980s and 1990s were as likely to work on the
strategy of total quality management (TQM, or TQ as others shortened it) as
upon empowerment. Surveys in the United States and Britain found, for example, that about three-quarters of large firms claim to have a TQM initiative in place (Mohrman et al. 1995; Wilkinson, Redman, and Snape 1993),
and the approach has spread to many European companies.

TQM works on several common themes. These include interventions to
increase product or service quality, personal growth of employees, empowerment, teamwork, and group and team leadership skills. Hill and Wilkinson
(1995) note the considerable confusion over just what TQM includes. They
distilled three major principles of customer orientation, process orientation,
and continuous improvement. The first signifies a focus on how to meet or
exceed the needs and expectations of customers. *Process* refers to a focus on
how groups are built into teams and linked most effectively within chains of
quality. *Continuous improvement* refers to a permanent quest within groups
and teams for ways to improve the product or services.

Research evidence on whether the TQM approaches, once built into an
organization, have significant impacts is sparse and contradictory, and has
generated more rhetorical debate than it has created knowledge. Paul Edwards,
Margaret Collinson, and Chris Rees, working for a British government agency
(1998) conducted a series of quantitative evaluations of six firms and agencies in an effort to show how evidence might best be developed and to yield
some authoritative findings regarding TQM. They found that employees
tended overall to approve of the TQM innovations and to believe that their
work roles had improved as a result of TQM adoption. They believed that
their teams had benefited from increased power to make decisions, but said
that this did not come with new levels of flexibility. Indeed, the old patterns
of supervisory monitoring and discipline went essentially unchanged. They

cite the aphorism that, "If you are going to be exploited, better that it is done well rather than badly." TQM is, the researchers found, not a strategy for dissolving the conflict inherent in worker-management relations but instead a means of managing it. Workers exhibited their knowledgeable awareness that, under TQM, they had to work harder and were more systematically controlled than before; thus, stress from the job was not reduced, but satisfaction with the mode of operations and increased confidence in the quality of the product or service was an outcome.

CORPORATE CULTURES

The concept of culture, though difficult to keep in focus and even more difficult to observe and measure, pertains to the belief system, behavior, values, and knowledge that make up the way of life of a people. The construct emphasizes the historically shared meanings, embodied in symbols, through which people cherish and communicate their life attitudes. Developed by anthropologists who pioneered in developing ethnological profiles of preliterate communities and societies, the culture concept was extended to a host of other human behavior settings. During the 1950s and 1960s, these included urban communities in industrial societies; during the 1970s, the idea was applied to organizations.

The application became a subfield of its own, within the arena of organizational behavior and human resource management, with the appearance of the very popular *In Search of Excellence* (1982), by the McKinsey firm consultants Thomas J. Peters and Robert H. Waterman. Their thesis, which they had begun to elaborate and refine in the 1970s, was that the excellence of a corporation was a function of its strength in creating a strong, unified culture based upon a shared vision.

There are a number of severe limitations in the field of organizational culture. One is that of "taxonomitus," as Peter Hawkins calls it (1997): the tendency to create definitional model after model and to build a literature that is primarily concerned with debates about conceptual definitions. An offshoot of this limitation is that fact that cultures are extremely difficult to bound intellectually. Do organizations within a national society, for instance, have genuinely separate cultures of their own? How does the sociological practitioner set a field research standard that allows her to test empirically and then conclude that a particular practice or thought way in a firm is indeed a kind of distinctive cultural characteristic? And if, as Talcott Parsons (1951) maintained, social systems and their subsystems in the structure of society form a kind of pyramid with culture at its base, personality and individual differences at its top, and society or social organization as the central mediator between the two, how much of what appears be cultural within an organization is in fact part of a more broadly generalized set of organized *social* relations?

Put differently, these limitations remind us that sociological practitioners improve their work and their service to clients to the extent that they can account for organizational outcomes in terms of social structures and relations. Another limitation arises in the course of applying culture as a construct to complex, formal organizations: If the practitioner does manage to validate or confirm the presence of a culture that inhibits organizational performance, renders it dysfunctional over time, or makes life miserable for its employees, how can the culture be changed? Kanter, Peters, Waterman, and other exponents of organizational restructuring emphasize the power relations among and within strata of employees and managers in corporations, and naturally their work is a call to senior executives to change the culture and remake it to fit the new models of empowerment and excellence. One set of culturalists distinguish somewhat between a corporate culture and an organization culture. In the former, managers presumably can alter the culture, somewhat at will, by eliminating old symbols, rites, and rituals, and injecting new meanings. Other types of organizations may lack a definite power hierarchy and have much more fluid boundaries.

Paul Bate (1994) copes valiantly with some of the conceptual and intervention dead-ends of the cultural approach. He states that "an organization culture, implying a second, unified entity, is pure myth"; that the notion of changing the whole organization, even through the heroic determination of chief officers, should be abandoned as a silly ambition. In his review of the possibilities for effective intervention, Bate cites the imposed, aggressive, top-down approach; the collaborative approach; and the training approach, among a few others. He concludes from his review that these exist only as corollary myths or as modes of consultative action that generally fail to work.

The corporate exemplars of a unified and well-communicated common culture, which have been explored by the practitioners of this approach and celebrated for their cultural ability to innovate and adapt to the challenge of change, have in some cases been overtaken and undermined by subsequent events. Terence E. Deal and Allan Kennedy, in their popular book, *Corporate Cultures* (1982), list among their exemplars Digital Equipment, which began its gradual collapse soon after 1982; Eastern Airlines, which went bankrupt and collapsed soon after the heroic chief executive Frank Borman came on the scene and did everything he could to rebuild the airline's culture; and Atari and Prime Computer, both computer hardware firms that were trampled by competitive "elephants" within a few years after 1982. Deal and Kennedy, like many other consultants of the culture era, also spent much of their intellectual capital on contrasting the Japanese corporate model with the American and suggesting that American firms could lose out permanently in global competition with Japan unless they found ways to change their cultures. By 1996, however, the Japanese corporate Rising Sun had set. My point is echoed by Deal and Kennedy themselves toward the end of their book: "Let's be candid about this. . . . Cultural change is still a black art as far as we are concerned" (Deal and Kennedy 1982, 164).

Undeterred by how little anyone knows about how to induce positive change, however, these authors offered a case of a public agency where they succeeded in consulting collaboratively and helping to induce such change on a noteworthy scale. The steps, as they summarized them, are:

1. Analyze key features of the agency and focus on those in greatest need of change.
2. Help put into position a hero who will take charge of the change process.
3. Find a valid threat to the future of the agency from the outside, such that survival is at stake.
4. Create transition rituals that permit employees to mourn the old ways and contrast them firmly with the new order.
5. Set up training operations to communicate the new ways accurately.
6. Bring in outside consultants to mediate some of the conflicts and to evaluate the resulting changes.
7. Create tangible symbols of the new ways.
8. Insist on job security throughout the change process.

This prescription, perhaps sound in itself, does not permit the consultant who adopts it to gauge whether it can be internalized by an organizational client. Nor does it offer clues to how substantial the external threat must be, for instance, before it induces the startup of the change process. It does not provide much guidance on the question of how heroic the change leader must be in order to carry the day, and it does little to explain how one measures whether the new culture, toward the close of the change process, will endure over time.

The newest and most volatile of industries in the United States today are those in the high-technology sector. The main locus for this industry is Silicon Valley in the San Francisco Bay metropolitan area. So great are the prospects for high capital gains in this industry, and so underdeveloped are the range of firms needed to support it when it matures, that there were approximately 2,000 would-be new firms starting up or trying to start in any year of the 1995–2000 period.

Some of the styles and rituals common in the high-technology Valley in the 1970s—"dress codes" based on Birkenstock sandals, T shirts, blue jeans, and (on cold days) denim jackets; flex hours; fraternity-style beer busts and sports teams, for example—appeared to be connected to the operating fortunes of the first firms. These can be thought of as *frozen commodities*: symbolic forms that emerge during sociocultural changes (such as those generated by the youth movements of the 1960s and early 1970s) and subsequently become fashions on the racks of every conventional retail outlet, which no longer signify commitment to social change.

The new firms in Silicon Valley started up around one or two hardware, software, or service innovations. Their initiators worked to attract investment capital. They then produced and sold for two or three years and watched to see whether a larger firm would buy them out or attach them as investments, or whether an initial public offering would be possible as the product began to sell. Most of the start-up firms failed. Those that succeeded tended to be acquired rapidly; as this occurred, employees were laid off and went in search of other start-ups. Surrounding a handful of Fortune 500 corporations, then, were thousands of little firms whose days were numbered in the hundreds. The big corporations put nearly all of their production operations into foreign labor markets and concentrated only their highest executive cadres and administrative support workers in the Valley.

There is a sense in which their distinctive cultures do not tell us a great deal about the growth or failures of the Silicon Valley firms, whether huge or start-up. Their prospects may hinge far more profoundly on product and service trends in the marketplaces of the world; on pricing and technical service support qualities; and on the symbolism of brands and brand advertising. They can flourish or die under heroes, tyrants, or playful yuppies. Some aspire to achieve the management-school design popular in the early 1990s: a corporation composed of just a few key decision makers, with every other function contracted out to some other work force. Under these conditions, employee loyalty, morale, vertical and horizontal communication networks, and the rites and rituals of company culture do not signify much, especially when compared with the cross-pressures of global competition and the search for new markets.

Among the start-ups and the smaller corporations, meanwhile, the executives zoom back and forth between opportunities in a search for stock options and quick acquisitions. Loyalty is more or less obsolete and even archaic, and the OD vision of taking years to build an effective and optimally productive organization is rendered immaterial. Kanter's emphasis upon employee participation and corporate flexibility, so central to the forces for positive change in the 1980s, began to dwindle toward insignificance in the high-technology sector a decade later.

Sociologist Vicki Smith, in her review called "New Forms of Work Organization," concluded that the participatory, flexible, and culture-changing emphases of developers such as Kanter and Peters and Waterman have "diffused throughout the American work and occupational system. . . . [T]he new model is pervasive, even if unevenly developed across . . . settings" (Smith 1997, 319). This is especially the case in sectors other than high technology, and has extended to include (somewhat reluctant) union acceptance in manufacturing and production settings.

Smith calls the organizational trends of the 1990s "downright confusing." She finds from a review of the research literature that decentralization of management, increased structural flexibility, and the movement downward of middle managerial authority and responsibility are all major trends of the era. However, they take place alongside much greater employment instability; intensification of worker tasks; and a rising division between regular employees, who are provided improved participation, training, and mobility opportunities, and temporary contract workers, who live outside this framework and have few if any of these perquisites of employment. The latter temporaries are, she reports, typically excluded from company events and rituals that build cohesiveness for others. Personnel cutbacks, downsizing, reduced wages, increased work obligations, and intra-firm job transfers are much more characteristic of the corporate workplace today than are upgrades in the interior culture.

OD professionals reflect in their own values and work concerns a rising division between the older ideals of sensitivity to the social side of organizations—to participation, quality of life concerns, morale, and security—and the new emphasis on organizational performance, productivity, and net profitability. The old ideals persist, a survey of OD practitioners revealed, but the new assignments are on the rise (Van Eynde et al. 1992), and many of those in the field are increasingly roped into the task of fitting the personnel (both line and managerial) into the changing technical systems of production, finance, marketing, and outsourcing, as opposed to humanization of the settings.

LEARNING ORGANIZATION THEORY

I have pointed out that a major problem with the culture-change and excellence and flexibility movements of the 1970s and 1980s was that the companies that appeared to exemplify the new developments have, for the most part, declined or failed. These movements were overtaken somewhat in the 1990s by the advent of the learning organization approach. This approach was formulated initially by Argyris and Schon (1987) and has been elaborated since then by Dunphy and Griffiths (1994), Pedlar et al. (1994), and many others. The preoccupation of this approach is with the search for ways to build *learning* capabilities into companies so that "action" research and development begin to take place as a project within a company, and thus, over time, build a capacity for positive change from within. The similarities between the long-standing tradition of action research in sociology and action projects in developing learning organizations are very strong, and Argyris is a major linking agent between the two (Argyris, Putnam, and Smith 1990).

There are, however, crucial conceptual difficulties with the learning construct. One is the question of whether change and learning differ much and, if so, just how. Another is whether learning is a behavior confined to individuals or something that can be generalized to whole organizations and even societies. A third is the absence of sufficient knowledge about the conditions under which learning begins and ends and what reversion comes into play in the aftermath. In spite of these difficulties, the learning approach represents another effort to embody OD work within a framework, in which the team of intervenors may propose something concrete that is then left in place as the team withdraws or limits its subsequent involvement. Certainly, the framework permits better presentation and explanation to corporate decision makers as to what actions will be entailed and how they may be built into the structure over time. Central to the learning approach is the notion of "double loop learning": the single loop is learning how to change operating subsystems of a corporation; the double loop includes this as well as vision and strategic actions overall. OD that deals narrowly with single loops, they say, will be of slight long-term utility (Argyris and Schon 1987).

OTHER APPLICATIONS

The kinds of concepts and interventions described in this chapter are not confined to research and development of corporations and companies. they have also been widely applied to schools, colleges and universities, religious organizations, and government agencies and the military. Sociological practitioners bring elements of OD—the use of behavioral science knowledge to improve both employee well-being and organizational effectiveness—to all these organizations.

Hundreds of examples could be presented, but I have chosen one because it expresses some of ways in which sociologists approach this field. Under contract with the National Institute of Education of the U.S. Department of Education, D. Catherine Baltzell and I conducted a study about selecting American school principals (Baltzell and Dentler 1983). It had two parts: one was a field study of how principals in that era were in fact appointed; the other was an interpretive set of developmental steps a school district could adopt to select principals intelligently and equitably. The notion of the National Institute professionals was that guidelines were needed to improve selection procedures, as a pivotal part of overall school improvement efforts. Two assumptions were made by the Institute officers in charge: That current practices were relatively ignorant and nonrational, and that sound practices of a quasi-scientific sort could be devised that would have reliability and predictive validity of quality when put to use.

In phase 1, our project team focused on describing common practices in principal selection. Using a quasi-ethnographic method of inquiry, field research teams from the project investigated selection practices in ten randomly sampled, geographically diverse school districts with 10,000 or more students. Cross-case analyses were then conducted to reveal variations and commonalities in the practices. In phase 2, we obtained nationwide nominations of districts with exemplary and alternative practices (as contrasted with conventional systems).

Contrary to the expectations of National Institute professionals and to most of the literature on school leadership, most of the recently appointed principals in the phase 1 sample had not been selected with a view to their managerial or instructional leadership abilities. These abilities were not expressed in vacancy announcements, nor did they appear in the selection criteria shared with the educators, administrators, and parents who took part in the screening. The conventional districts—eight in ten of those studied—sought out white candidates who were already known to and esteemed by administrators and influential citizens in the district. The men who were chosen were most often very tall and looked impressive in three-piece suits; many others were white women, who were usually chosen to be principals of elementary schools. In short, district influentials knew full well how they found and appointed school principals. The process worked within a long-established social network of very local educators who were appointed because they showed the best fit with the subculture of the district and its surrounding community.

In the innovative districts, diversity was stressed, not as a virtue in itself, but as an inevitable outcome of selecting persons who were managerial and educational leaders. These few districts publicized their searches to a larger array of outside groups, and often networks of outstanding teachers would signal to one another that an opening had been posted and that the selection process would be focusing on leadership abilities.

The process was, in either instance, rational in that it generated appointments of just the sorts of principals that superintendents, school board members, and politically influential members of the supporting communities wanted. In the conventional districts, the process was of long standing, understood by all participants, and localistic in style and history, yet very similar to the process used in hundreds of surrounding districts.

Districts innovated in their searches for educational leaders only when some very threatening event had taken place. Change was a function of a substantial, widely recognized threat to the viability or integrity of the district. This included bankruptcy, financial and sexual scandals, court-ordered remedies, takeovers by state education authorities, threats of merger into other districts, and the like. At such junctures, moreover, superintendents and board members had no difficulty setting up procedures that generated highly qualified, leadership-tested, and gender- and ethnically diverse candidates. National associations of school administrators were at the time demonstrating and advocating for assessment centers where prospective principals and other administrators could be tested and trained for leadership, and asking that the ratings of those assessed be shared with school superintendents. Our study included visits to two of these centers as part of phase 2.

Our project produced two volumes, one a research monograph and the second a manual for developing within any district an effective, rational, equitable, and documentable selection procedure. The second volume was in fact superfluous. Very few requests for copies and far fewer contacts for consultative assistance came in, because Americans were already fully capable of devising and installing techniques for finding and selecting principals. They simply differed from community to community on what sorts of teachers and administrators they wished to employ, and the differences were expressions of long-held values and attitudes. Indeed, one district in California had two selection procedures on its shelf. One was a paper procedure, so well thought out and technically so fair and precise in locating educational leaders that its chief author, the personnel director, moonlighted as a consultant to other districts about how to devise and install this exemplary procedure. The same director, at the same time, managed the procedure actually used in his district. It entailed grooming "good old boys," as he termed them, who could then be helped to pass a test interview and to write an acceptable essay, and who knew in advance that they would be appointed as vacancies came up. These were, with few exceptions, white male graduates from the same neighboring college.

Our study also found that principals of public schools are not at all uniformly pivotal to the success or failure of their schools as learning environments. In perhaps a fifth of schools, they are crucial to positive effectiveness, but in most schools they simply reflect, symbolize, and help to deliver whatever the power elites of the community desire. If public expectations about the quality of service from local public agencies (including schools) tend to be low, then principals were not encouraged to contradict this set of expectations, and might be replaced if they tried. In some instances, teachers empowered one another, ignoring what teachers in one of the schools called "the tall suit in the front office," and built their own improvements into the daily events of the learning environment.

In other instances, little more than advance grooming and networks of buddies-as-advocates made up the way in which administrators of *all* public agencies were selected. What would have had to change, we found, was the set of value preferences shared by the community—a change the National Institute of Education was not authorized to try to implement. In fact, the Reagan administration found a way to disestablish the Institute itself just three years after the project was completed.

CONCLUSION

Theories and social research about complex, formal organizations are a century old. The efforts to utilize the theories began in the 1920s, grew substantially during the 1930s, and became a solid, enduring part of all of the social and behavioral sciences during and after World War II. As applications became more universal, they migrated out of academic departments of sociology and psychology and became increasingly consolidated into departments of behavioral organization within schools of management.

Although psychologists predominate in organization development, the key concepts for and approaches to inducing change in organizations are an intellectual legacy of sociology. Central to all the work reviewed in this chapter is the idea of social relations within and between groups and of organizations as composed of stratified, bounded teams made up of interlocking groups. Bureaucracy, oligarchy, and other forms of structural dominance are also parts of the sociological heritage. Over the past several decades of activity within OD, however, notions about the boundaries of academic disciplines have tended to erode, as highly applied practitioners came together from diverse intellectual and scientific fields to collaborate on the analysis, diagnosis, and treatment of organizations. In the latter sense, and as the contributions of the Tavistock Institute make clear, the underlying mode of action is clinical: for example, observational scrutiny, differentiation of the pathological within the system, prognosis, and a strategy of treatment that requires enlistment of the participants themselves for implementation.

Today, the larger and more complex organizations become, the more they tend to include trainers and developers on their own staffs, or to retain them in the same way they retain law firms, medical services, and accountants. Indeed, the largest accounting firms in each Western nation have full-time OD specialists and consultants on their staffs, available as experts for projects within client organizations. The determiners of the process are almost always senior managers. In the U.S. Army, corporals do not make plans and policies, generals do. So, too, in business and industry, the call for OD assistance may begin in the human resources division or department, but it lodges sooner rather than later with the chief executive officer.

As a result, some of the social idealism in OD, so prominent in the focus on employee mental health, job security, and work satisfaction, has given way to the pressing concerns of production, customer service, and system performance. In nonprofit organizations such as churches and religious groups, the same trend is apparent, as the professional leader aims OD at increasing membership and building a better stream of annual giving. In higher education, OD is asked to focus on building and retaining enrollments, restructuring to reduce operating costs, and devising methods for intensifying accountability. Senior administrators are seldom much interested in what would improve the happiness of professors.

OD, and related specialty fields of reviving, enabling, or revising organizations, were once uncommon participants on the social landscape. Today, they are very numerous and observably active. Virtual industries of consultants vie within business for opportunities to undertake projects. This chapter has offered only a few examples of the many approaches that compete for attention and produce new concepts and terms of art every few years. There are thirteen periodicals devoted to topics of organizational analysis and OD, and hundreds more publications come from individual corporations and institutions reporting on their alleged attainments in restructuring themselves.

As with other domains of sociological practice, both valid and reliable research and successful interventions or technical assistance are extremely difficult to carry out. As the complexity of organizational life multiplies exponentially, so the complexity of reflexive understanding and strategic induction of planned change is increased. In the years from 1900 to 1925, government lawyers and senior civil servants who went on travel assignments often observed the courtesy of stopping by the White House on their ways out and back to leave calling cards and notes indicating their plans. In the 1990s, in contrast, Vice President Albert Gore led a task force that worked for five years on "Reinventing Government," searching for ways to limit agency growth, reduce paperwork, and increase efficiency. Ironically, during those years, the number of personnel employed by the federal government actually increased.

Organizational analysis plays a part in every intervention practitioners undertake. Each social policy spawns a policy organization that hosts programs, whether the domain is crime prevention and control, drug and alcohol rehabilitation services, child abuse control, or the structure of intergovernmental communications. OD is no more or less successful than many other efforts to practice in these and similar fields. Does psychotherapy work? Do support groups have measurable, positive results? Do schools educate? Today's social service systems and delivery mechanisms are subject to increasingly profound challenges, as they are overtaken by rapid changes in their settings and environments and as they are found, when scrutinized, to have based their activities on (social) scientifically dubious premises in the first place. Get-tough laws grounded in cultural assumptions about criminal deterrence are but one illustration.

Assumptions by senior officials about their ability to manage organizations from the top down provide another illustration of what often fails to be sufficient today. When the oil freighter *Exxon Valdez* crashed on the shores of Alaska (as described in chapter 2), what we had before us from the OD viewpoint was a very big problem in corporate organizational analysis: What procedures and failed safeguards combined to make this tragic accident possible? This OD question arose long before sociology dealt with the affected community facing the disaster brought them by Exxon.

At the turn of the century, as OD matures, it has new and increasingly strong tools of inquiry and treatment in its kit, but it continues to face stubborn avoidance and strong resistance from within organizations of all kinds. What leaders of any bureaucracy are disposed to turn inward and examine their problems and introduce ways to solve them? University managers and faculties, for example, are vastly more skilled at identifying problems and recommending solutions to others than they are at examining the efficacy of their own activities.

Still, conscious, intentional, mandated change is now part of the organizational ethos. It is often trumpeted in advertisements and bragged about as a point in an organization's favor, even when the change is shallow and results in very little. Today's student of sociological practice will find that knowledge about theories and techniques of organizational analysis and intervention is essential to her professional life and work, whether as a realm of practice or as a matter of contextual comprehensiveness for her own career and prospects for control and autonomy.

REFERENCES

Argyris, C., and D. A. Schon. 1987. *Organizational Learning: A Theory in Action Perspective*. Reading, Mass.: Addison Wesley.

Argyris, C., R. Putnam, and D. M. Smith. 1990. *Action Science*. San Francisco: Jossey-Bass.

Baltzell, D. C., and R. A. Dentler. 1983. *Selecting American School Principals: A Research Report*. Cambridge, Mass.: Abt Associates Inc.

Bate, P. 1994. *Strategies for Cultural Change*. Oxford: Butterworth-Heinemann Ltd.

Bruhn, J. G. 1997. The organization as a person: Analogues for intervention. *Clinical Sociological Review* 15: 51–70.

Cooley, C. H. 1909 (reprint 1962). *Social Organization*. New York: Schocken.

Cullen, J. 1998. The needle and the damage done: Research, action research, and organizational and social construction of health in the "Information Society." *Human Relations* 51: 154–64.

Deal, T. E., and A. A. Kennedy. 1982. *Corporate Cultures: The Rites and Rituals of Corporate Life*. Reading, Mass.: Addison Wesley.

Dunphy, D. C., and A. Griffiths. 1994. *Theories of Organizational Change as Models for Intervention*. Paper No. 043, Center for Corporate Change, Australian Graduate School of Management. University of New South Wales.

Dyer, W. 1994. *Team Building: Issues and Alternatives*. Reading, Mass.: Addison Wesley.

Edwards, P., M. Collinson, and C. Rees. 1998. The determinants of employee responses to Total Quality Management. *Organization Studies* 19, no. 3: 449–76.

Hawkins, P. April 1997. Organizational culture: Sailing between evangelism and complexity. *Human Relations* 50, no. 4: 417–24.

Hill, S., and A. Wilkinson.1995. In search of TQM. *Employee Relations* 17, no. 3: 8–25.

Hiller, E. T., ed. 1928. *The Strike*. Chicago: University of Chicago Press.

Johnson, R. D., and E. K. Thurston. 1997. Achieving empowerment using the empowerment strategy grid. *Leadership and Organization Development Journal* 18, no. 2: 64–74.

Kanter, R. M. 1983. *The Change Masters: Innovation for Productivity in the American Corporation*. New York: Simon & Schuster.

Kets de Vries, M. F. R. et al. 1991. *Organizations on the Couch*. San Francisco: Jossey-Bass.

Lawler, E. E., S.A. Mohrman, and G. E. Ledford. 1992. *Employee Involvement in Total Quality Management: Practice and Results in Fortune 1000 Companies*. San Francisco: Jossey-Bass.

Levinson, H. 1972. *Organizational Analysis*. Cambridge, Mass.: Harvard University Press.

Link, H. C. 1918. *Employment Psychology*. New York: Macmillan.

Mayo, E., and G. F. F. Lombard. 1944. *Teamwork and Labor Turnover in the Aircraft Industry of Southern California*. Harvard Business Research Studies No. 32. Cambridge, Mass.: Harvard Graduate School of Business Administration.

McGregor, D. 1960. *The Human Side of Enterprise.* New York: McGraw-Hill.

Miller, D. C., and W. H. Form. 1980. *Industrial Sociology: Work in Organizational Life.* 3d ed. New York: Harper & Row.

Mohrman, S. A., R. V. Tenkas, E. E. Lawler, and G. E. Ledford. 1995. Total Quality Management: Practice and outcomes in the largest US firms. *Employee Relations* 17, no. 3: 26–40.

Parsons, T. 1951. *The Social System.* Glencoe, Ill: Free Press.

Pedlar, M., J. G. Burgoyne, and T. Boydell. 1994. *Towards the Learning Company: Concepts and Practices.* London: McGraw-Hill.

Peters, T. J., and R. H. Waterman. 1982. *In Search of Excellence.* New York: Harper & Row.

Schaef, A. W., and D. Fassel. 1988. *The Addictive Organization.* San Francisco: Harper & Row.

Smith, V. 1997. New forms of work organization. *Annual Review of Sociology* 23: 315–40.

Taylor, F. W. 1911. *The Principles of Scientific Management.* New York: Harper & Row.

Trist, E., and H. Murray II. 1990. *The Social Engagement of Science.* vol. 1. Philadelphia: Pennsylvania Press.

Van Eynde, D. F., A. Church, R. F. Hurley, and W. W. Burke. 1992. What old practitioners believe. *Training and Development* 46, no.4: 41–45.

Wilkinson, A., T. Redman, and E. Snape. 1993. *Quality and the Manager.* London: Institute of Management.

4

Work and Labor Relations

INTRODUCTION

The study of work and industrialization has been part of sociology since its emergence in the nineteenth century. Social class structures and relations became a focus of theory and analysis for Karl Marx and later Emile Durkheim and Max Weber and their colleagues; much of this interest was an offshoot of the rise of industrialism in Western societies. In chapter 3 I focused on the ways in which sociologists today practice within and between complex, formal organizations. It should be obvious, however that there are few boundaries between this realm of practice and the realm of industrial relations, labor relations, work, and unions.

This chapter should therefore be read as a continuation of chapter 3, with the addition here of some categories of content not covered there. In keeping with the expanding role of sociological practice in the economies and societies of the world beyond the United States, practice in projects involving work and labor relations now extends to whole sectors of economic development and associated social and political changes in the global economy.

BEGINNINGS

Macro-social change results mainly from changes in the technology of work, in the amount and targeting of capital investments, and in the subcultures of occupations. It follows from this that great changes often take place during upheavals such as wars and economic depressions. The enormous role of technological change is often exemplified by the turn-of-the-century assembly lines introduced into meat-packing plants in Chicago and Cincinnati between 1900 and 1910. The overhead trolleys devised to convey carcasses along the packing-house floor caught the eye of Henry Ford, who designed an auto assembly line that began operations in 1913. His design reduced the time required to assemble a chassis from 12.5 man-hours to 93 man-minutes. Automobile, truck, and engine manufacture grew exponentially during World War I, and that technology began to be adapted to manufacturing processes of many kinds.

Workers on assembly lines soon became the worldwide models for those who were oppressed, deskilled—that is, stripped of the opportunity to learn and use craft skills in their work—and bored or dispirited to death. During the Great Depression of the 1930s, millions of workers throughout the Western world were laid off, displaced, and relocated, and became the objects of massive government welfare programs as industrial capitalism staggered toward economy-wide bankruptcy. In reaction, workers in thousands of businesses and industries swelled the ranks of existing unions and created many new ones.

In the United States, twentieth-century unionism became established from within the American Federation of Labor (AFL), which was formed by clusters of skilled craft and trade workers. It grew from roughly half a million members in 1900 to about 4 million in 1920, mainly under the stimulus of war mobilization and governmental backing from the Woodrow Wilson administration. This growth was followed by sharp declines during the 1920s, however, when corporate and political elites turned against the AFL and against the International Workers of the World, a union movement intended to enlist unskilled workers. By the eve of the Great Depression in 1929, the AFL had been reduced to the half-million level it had attained in 1900. During the Depression, unionism enjoyed a resurgence of political support, and John L. Lewis of the United Mine Workers succeeded in creating the Congress of Industrial Organizations (CIO) to accommodate the growing numbers of semi-skilled workers. With the tremendous production stimulus of World War II, total union membership grew to 15 million. Governmental support for unions was instrumental to that growth; this support was, in important measure, the result of a tradeoff in which union leaders pledged not to strike, to protect the war effort, if the government would back collective bargaining and organizing efforts of all kinds.

The climate for unions in the United States became grim in the 1980s and continued to be grim in the 1990s (Ettore 1993). Thomas Geoghegen (1992) believes the downturn began with the advent of the Taft-Hartley Act of 1947, and so his account of the demise of unions differs from that of other scholars. Membership now stands at about 16 percent of the employed work force— dropping to 11 percent among private-sector workers. Contrast these figures with those from 1956, when private-sector membership rose to 35 percent. With downsizings, layoffs, automation, and consolidations in manufacturing plants, most unions' membership numbers have declined drastically. Auto worker membership stood at 1.5 million in 1975; today, a quarter of a century later, it is about 850,000. Steelworker union members that previously numbered 1.4 million are now less than 700,000; machinists, not long ago numbering 1 million members, now have fewer than 650,000.

Under the Reagan and Bush administrations, the National Labor Board issued rules that favored management, notably one restricting on-site union organizing and permitting the permanent replacement of striking workers. Ettore quotes Harvard labor economist Richard Freeman, who is essentially an ally of unionism, as forecasting that by the year 2000 only 5 percent of workers in the private sector would be unionized (Ettore 1993). A labor lawyer, Thomas Geoghegan, wrote this:

Organized labor. Say those words, and your heart sinks. I am a labor lawyer, and my heart sinks. . . . This is my cause. But these days it's too old, too arthritic, to be a cause. . . . It is a mastodon of a thing, crawling off to Bal Harbour to die. . . . Sometimes, as a mental exercise, I try to think of the A.F.L.-C.I.O. in the year 2001. But I cannot do it. The whole idea is too perverse. U.S. manufacturing has gone down . . . the drain, and with it, it seems, the entire labor movement. Just 16 percent of the workforce now, down from 20 to 24 percent 10 years ago. Maybe it will drop to 12. Once it drops to 10, it might as well keep dropping to 0. (Geoghegan 1992, 12)

In spite of this general trend toward the demise of unions in the United States, there are signs of a modest comeback since 1993. Union membership declined overall from 22 million in 1975 to 16.4 million in 1992, but in

1993 it showed its first slight resurgence, rising to 16.6 million, and this trend persisted for several years. There has been some new success in organizing unions among white-collar, service, and government workers. The two largest teachers' unions; the state, county, and municipal unions; and private-sector service workers' unions have all shown some growth, although manufacturing unions have continued to shrink. New leadership in the mine workers' union and in the Teamsters has begun to generate some renewed growth.

A number of pro-union leaders, including Stanford University law professor William Gould and Fred Feinsten, another labor lawyer, were appointed by President Clinton at the start of his administration in 1993. However, Congress refused to pass any union-facilitating legislation, thereby dashing the new hopes of union leaders. Clinton endorsed a bill that would have ended the use of replacement workers during strikes, for example, and another that would have strengthened worker health and safety rules, but these never became law. The idea that unionism would be revived under a Democratic Party executive administration was not fulfilled, although that political change did trigger some new prospects for parts of the labor movement. Unfortunately for unions, the advent of the second Bush administration may well signal a return to the anti-union strategies of the 1908s.

Arthur B. Shostak, a practicing sociologist who has studied, written about, and advised labor unions for forty years, disagrees. He is hard at work guiding unions into becoming "CyberUnions" (Shostak 1999). He projects a future in which all unions and all members will be in contact with one another through the Internet to poll members, exchange new ideas, devise new ways to carry out their missions within firms and other organizations, and put themselves into cyberspace in all respects.

Shostak does not believe that this is a silver bullet for unions' problems; rather, he sees it as a powerful stimulus when combined with political action, robust organizing, and the other mass-movement techniques of the 1930–1950 era. He works to encourage unions to install full computer capabilities both internally and among themselves, through his role as an "Adjunct Sociologist" at the National Labor College and its AFL-CIO George Meany Center for Labor Studies. His fear as a futurist and planner is that unions will become organizational and industrial anachronisms unless they adapt to and incorporate the full array of computer and communications technologies into their structures.

Shostak's work with unions pursues the ideal of building union strength through developing member participation. As Renaud Paquet and Jean-Guy Bergeron (1996) noted, "The level of member participation in the union, the behavioral component of union commitment, is a prime concern of labor organizations. The effectiveness of union recruitment drives, collective bargaining, and political action is often directly proportional to the level of membership commitment." Their empirical survey of a representative sample of union members of the Public Service Alliance of Canada revealed that union participation is a function of job satisfaction, attitude toward the union and involvement with it, and co-worker participation. Involvement hinges mainly on each worker's estimate of the functionality, or instrumental exchange value, of participation; but it is also shaped by each worker's feelings of attachment toward the union itself. Conflict with management in itself is not predictive of union participation.

Working from a similar perspective, sociologist Richard Kronish has used his economic and sociological expertise in assisting unions for more than a quarter of a century. He began in 1973 by lecturing automobile workers and union leaders in the United Auto Workers on the implications of the multinational activities of their managers and corporations, focusing on the English-U.S. relationship in particular. This was *pro bono* work that grew out of his studies in international economics. As his union involvements ripened, he was soon asked to consult with the trade unions as to optimal investment of union-generated member pensions.

Kronish, who earned his Ph.D. at the University of Wisconsin at Madison in the 1960s, said he learned in those years that a sociologist was supposed to make use of his discipline in the service of groups in the larger society, and that this had been one of his reasons for choosing graduate study in sociology rather than economics. He found that trade union pension investments generally suffered from low return rates and reflected essentially pro-management policies. Following his study of pension fund investments, Kronish organized and ran two conferences at his campus, the University of Massachusetts at Boston, on social investments and their prospects. He also set up a local demonstration project on this topic for contractors and members of the Carpenters Union within the Boston District Council.

Deepening this involvement, Kronish helped the Council to invest in selected building and real estate ventures and continued to teach union leaders about investment strategies. This participation became so substantial that

Kronish took a two-thirds leave from teaching and other faculty duties for seven years during the 1970s, a time when carpenters and other builders were facing shrinking markets in New England and discovering that labor strikes were generally no longer effective tools for shaping collective bargaining. He worked to build educational opportunities for young carpenters into the Council system; gave technical assistance on issues of racial and ethnic diversification of the union membership at its entry point; put in skills-training arrangements for women and minorities, for building-trades jobs; and continued to advise on investment questions. The diversity efforts at training collapsed when a regional recession began in 1988. As the only social scientist on the Council staff, Kronish also focused on achieving tax exemptions for education and training and on methods for refinancing facilities.

In collaboration with leaders of the Carpenters Union and with lawyers retained for the purpose, Richard Kronish designed and put into operation a bank capable of financing mortgages for union members and others. It was called the First Trade Union Savings Bank and was funded by union pension funds. He then joined the new bank as a leader on its investment committee and as an operations monitor, but did not become a bank employee. Later he became chair of the bank's board of directors. Eventually the bank succeeded in investing in low-income housing.

In Kronish's view, sociological training has aided his union practice in several ways; quantitative and analytic skills, applied mathematics, social survey techniques, and organization-building skills have all helped greatly. More importantly, he believes, sociology schooled him in how to formulate an issue and how to look beneath its surface for interpretation. He never approached his role in unions as a research observer and has written only once about union events. In recent years, he has begun to transfer these experiences into medical care and diagnostic settings, finding that the same sociological training helps him to grasp the sociology of health care systems.

Shostak and Kronish are alike in their practical focus upon strengthening the scope and quality of member and leader participation in unions. There are countless cross-pressures in the political and economic environments that surround labor unions, and many of these are hostile and negative; nonetheless, these sociological practitioners have worked on ways to make unions what Shostak calls more robust. The means utilized are most often through commitment to innovate programmatically in ways that will hold and attract members.

There are some signs of a revival in American unionism. Labor economist

Michael D. Yates (1997) depicted a major turnover in the top electoral leadership in 1995 as a sign of revitalization. William Foote Whyte and Joseph R. Blasi (1984, 139) reviewed the prospects for growth of employee ownership in the United States and the relationship of such ownership to traditional unionism. They concluded:

There are now over 500 majority employee-owned companies in the United States and over 5,000 minority employee-owned companies. The phenomenon is growing rapidly. . . . Unions can either watch this phenomenon or guide it. There are levels of choice and involvement open to them. Employee ownership can be seen as one tool, part of a general policy on plant shutdowns.

CURRENT TRENDS

In thousands of business enterprises throughout the world, and thus throughout labor forces and union groups, the current management quest is for adaptations to economic globalization. Expressive of this quest is the story of the formation of the Latin American Sociology of Work Association, spearheaded by Lais Abrama and associates (1997). The group was unable to obtain funding for its cross-national study projects, yet a number of the projects within the larger whole were completed.

Industrial and business firms alike are substantially smaller in corporate scope and workforce scale in Latin American economies. Some 300 sociologists came together to rejuvenate a previously lagging applied sociology of work there in the last decade. Their efforts draw on labor/economic theories from the United States and England, but are distinctive in their essential focus on the symbolic interactions of workers within segments of industry and within unions. (Macro-economic and demographic approaches are much more common in the postindustrial economies to the north.)

Consistent with the theoretical orientation described in this book, the Brazilian sociologists who studied union responses to the technological changes sweeping through the industries of that country took "worker subjectivity" in the face of the change process very seriously. Brazil is well ahead of other economies of Latin America in the advent of these changes; what the sociologists inferred from their first phase of research was that both psychosocial ambiguities in worker response and gender, age, and skill-level differences in disposition made planning for a cross-national union strategy very difficult. In several other countries where globalization was studied, the focus of the projects was on worker perceptions of changes in the content of their work and on the worker-machine relationship.

The concerns regarding globalization and technological change faced by practitioners in Latin America are widely shared in other countries. For two decades, the most advanced industrial countries of Europe and North America have faced the question of whether an industrial relations system transformation is taking place. Christopher L. Erickson and Sarash Kuruvilla (1998) reviewed the evidence and the literature surrounding this debate. Such a debate is both important and customary in the course of applying the social sciences. It is the equivalent of asking, in program evaluation research, whether the program addresses a social problem—before examining the theory of the program strategy itself.

The first finding in the Erickson and Kuruvilla review was that those engaged in the debate do not define *transformation* in the same way. Diverse clues are offered: decentralization in collective bargaining, management's increased autonomy, worker teams, flex time, job assignment flexibility, to name just a few of the presumed sources of change. Other analysts focus on wage pattern changes, changes in laws and regulations, and more institutional features. Social scientists, in short, cannot agree with each other about what a valid set of indicators of a noteworthy transformation of industrial relations might be.

There is no doubt that a very substantial number of business and industrial changes are taking place worldwide, but the settings are so diverse, and the rates of change so varied, that the vast canvas of industrial relations and labor organizations cannot be painted accurately as a single picture. The postindustrial revolution that is sweeping the globe cannot yet be graphed or timed or depicted reliably, just as no one could have foretold with accuracy the scope, pace, or full nature of the first industrial revolution. We only know that we are in it and that it has been evolving since World War II. One of the roles of applied sociologists of work and labor is to collaborate with others in trying to take the measure of this inordinately complex process and to predict its future course and consequences.

CHANGES IN WORK ROLES

British sociologists have been studying the ways in which work roles are changing as a result of globalism and technology as well as management strategies. In a review of their efforts, Douglas Ezzy wrote that Frederick Taylor and Henry Ford, the designers of the mass-production labor systems common to the first half of the twentieth century, assumed that "most workers preferred mindless labor. Ford argued that managers should control the organization of work and that most workers were dumb, stupid, and should be treated like animals" (1997, 431). Labor sociologists call this doctrine, so central to labor relations from 1910 through 1940, *Fordism*. Ezzy concluded that a newer form of management has substituted for Fordism a type of normative control through which the worker's experiences and feelings lead him to regard his work as part of the subjective self, as opposed to a set of tasks he carries out for a wage.

Two directions are taking form. In one, corporations today seek to manipulate the worker's view of self by injecting the symbols of the company into the identifications of the individuals who work there. This can take place both in advanced, high-technology settings such as Microsoft and in unskilled work forces such as McDonald's. In contrast, a secondary work force composed of temporaries and outsourced job contractors, in which workers remain insecure and where identity cannot be forged, is growing yearly. In either direction, the older pattern of a job for life is being eliminated. Some workers may benefit from this by devising ways to gain new and refreshing experience and to render their work duties more flexible. Others, including those with occasional periods of unemployment and those in the temp force, suffer from a schism between their idea of adulthood as grounded in a job and their actual path of experience.

For millions of workers in advanced, postindustrial settings, work itself is not dirty, hazardous, and alienating as it was in the era of Marx and his turn-of-the-century disciples. It may not even be oppressive, though it appears so to Harry Braverman (1974) in his widely cited work devoted to updating the Marxian perspective. Nevertheless, new forces within enterprises and across the global economy overall make workers in most situations today more harried, uncertain, and anxious.

COMPUTERIZATION

Among the forces inducing changes in work and labor relations, none is more influential than the technology of computerization. Beverly H. Burris (1998), in her review of sociological thinking and evidence on this generalization, confirmed the magnitude of the influence but did little else. The reports she reviewed are contradictory. Some social scientists report that the transformation of production triggered by computerization has promoted strong trends toward deskilling of the labor process and reduced worker autonomy. Others report an increase in managerial decentralization and a reduction in hierarchy, upskilling of work, and new value placed on the pivotal role of knowledge workers. A third set of reports says that the terrain has not yet been mapped and that any generalizations may be misleading. In short, we do not yet know precisely what we are talking about, because the scale of employment settings in the U.S. economy alone—never mind the rest of the world—is too vast and too varied to be mapped accurately.

There is some agreement among applied sociologists on at least one effect of computerization: Traditional rank authority has been reduced in status and power in work settings, yielding to the rise of knowledge and technical expertise. The engineer, the computer systems analyst, and the automator of accounting operations are among the many kinds of employees who tend now to be on a level with senior management, further separating the semi-skilled and support workers from influence.

Burris concluded that causal interpretations of the great influence of computerization on work are exceptionally hard to come by because the technological change is "embedded in a constellation of factors: the internalization of the division of labor, intensified worldwide competition, [and] . . . expanded need (and capacity) to manage complex organizations . . . and to perfect long-range planning" (1998, 52). It is also true that the culture of the workplace, often established in advance of computerization, defines the ways in which the technology will be put to use. A company firmly entrenched in Fordism, which manages through a hierarchy of fear, will utilize computerization to increase its managerial span of control and to further deskill lower-level workers. A company disposed toward a flat, decentralized structure with a culture of solidarity will utilize it to increase employee participation and co-involvement. The process is so complex, however, that these ingredients often do not coalesce in this intuitively attractive way.

RESTRUCTURING AND LAYOFFS

However the revolution taking place in businesses is interpreted, it has certain fairly common effects on U.S. employees. Corporations struggling to enlarge their market share and improve their net profitability have, in thousands of instances over the past decade, moved to restructure their firms and, as part of this set of changes, laid off workers. Layoffs are so common that journalists and managers do not use the term much any more, preferring the more neutral term *downsizing*. One labor analyst calculated that, in the first quarter of 1994 alone, 3,100 U.S. workers were laid off each day (Byrne 1994). Projected, this would equal more than 1 million layoffs per year! Furthermore, thousands of firms do not downsize once in a decade; they may repeat the process three or four times over a five-year period. In their report on this process, Elmer H. Burack and Robert P. Singh noted that:

Downsizing is forcing employees and employers to redefine their roles and expectations. . . . Older employment relationships and expectations have been destroyed. Stable full-time positions are disappearing, while the numbers of part-time and temporary workers continue to increase. . . . With the ever-changing corporate landscape, the confusion and demoralization of existing workers are understandable. Many employees do not know what is expected of them. The very meaning of the word "job" is changing. . . . Since the job helps define individuals in terms of widely recognized societal norms, the search for meaning in work and a basis for a new employment relationship becomes imperative to employer and employee alike. Few have strategically considered what new employment relationships will emerge. (1995, 13)

JOB DISSATISFACTION AND WORK REFORM

Sociologist Robert A. Rothman (1987) noted that sociologists have long been concerned with the nature and sources of job dissatisfaction among workers, and with the ways in which reforms in working conditions might ameliorate that dissatisfaction. Medical sociologists have often documented the correlations between job stresses and dissatisfactions and health problems of many kinds. Deskilled, dull, repetitive, seemingly meaningless tasks on the job, moreover, have often been assumed to reduce sharply the quality of lives in every industrialized economy. Rothman warns that measuring levels of job dissatisfaction is a complicated and error-ridden task, because of the tremendous variation in occupational subcultures within a national economy, and because the nature of the questions may generate denial or other self-protective responses from workers.

A Lou Harris poll taken in 1987 (Modic 1987) found that a national sample of American office workers were less likely to feel that the quality of their working life was improving (56 percent) than did their counterparts in 1978 (70 percent). The same workers were less likely to equate doing a good job with getting what they wanted out of life: 62 percent in 1978 versus 56 percent in 1987. Harris explained the shift on the basis of rising expectations among workers. The 1987 sample wanted to be challenged in their jobs, to participate in decision making, to communicate, to contribute, and to take responsibility for getting the job done. Their managers did not support these aims, and most of them did not allow fulfillment of these expectations and desires, according to the survey responses. In fact, most of the managers did not think that workers cared much about these attributes of work. The survey thus revealed a substantial gap between the workers' asserted expectations and the likelihood of delivery by supervisors.

Job dissatisfaction today is frequently a byproduct of intensification of competitiveness for businesses. Increases in workloads, frequent changes in duties, and fear of job loss combine, under the constant threat of downsizing, mergers, and reorganizations, to manifest themselves as diminished morale among skilled workers. In many companies, the key to success is a well-motivated work force that is able to deliver high-quality customer service. As morale drops, however, the key no longer turns, and managers striving to become more competitive are caught in self-defeating spirals.

As businesses have undergone great changes in recent decades, dissatisfactions often build into stresses of other kinds for workers. A 1996 poll released by Marketdata Enterprises (Dutton 1998) found that 5 percent of the 1,000 professionals who responded said they experienced "great stress" on a daily basis; another one-third indicated that this occurred more than twice a week for them. For the work force as a whole, Dutton reported that mental stress absences accounted for 1 percent of worker absences in 1996, double the rate for 1995. She cited data from the American Institute of Stress that estimate the cost for U.S. employers of absenteeism, employee turnover, direct medical costs, worker's compensation, and legal fees at roughly $250 billion annually. Some stress is inherent in the terms and conditions of work, of course, but the components that have risen sharply over the past decade appear to be the result of rising expectations among corporate leaders that everyone should do everything better, faster, and cheaper.

The major stressors that appear under these circumstances spring from bearing responsibility while lacking authority, an inability to voice complaints, poor working conditions, inadequate recognition, and insecurity about job stability. Ironically, the American response, when there is one, is to offer exercise rooms, workshops on breathing and meditation, and behavioral-medicine training in relaxation. These palliatives work for many employees in the short term, but they do not directly address the structural sources of stress. A more fundamental remedy is suggested by the work of two social scientists who reported on an experiment with a more structural intervention. Rick D. Hackett and Peter Bycio, knowing that employee absenteeism had been estimated in 1990 to cost the North American economy billions in lost productivity each year, evaluated a medical practice in which nurses were given a day of absence from work on an average of once every other month. Data were kept on the effects on their physical and mental health. Hackett and Bycio obtained convincing evidence of improvements in the nurses' health as a result of the self-scheduled absences. In short, a stressful occupation could still yield a significant improvement in well-being if absences were built into the work schedule (Hackett and Bycio 1996).

In any event, we have abundant survey evidence to show that three out of four professional and managerial job holders express satisfaction with their jobs, whereas job holders in unskilled occupations express the lowest levels of satisfaction. Generally, on average on a four-point scale, the unskilled worker is three-quarters of a point less satisfied than the professional. We also know that this pattern holds for both sexes and for minority groups as well as whites.

Sources of dissatisfaction were divided by Rothman into extrinsic and intrinsic types (Rothman 1987). The extrinsic factors include earnings, safety and health, and work content items such as hours. Intrinsic factors include opportunities for autonomy, challenge, skill utilization, and self-expression. When managerial and professional workers express dissatisfaction, it tends heavily to be about extrinsic factors; but when other workers say they are dissatisfied, their complaints are often about the intrinsic. Obviously, this is a reflection on the nature of the work roles themselves, in which self-fulfillment and autonomy of any kind are least likely to come from an unskilled job.

One direct approach to reforming the workplace in the 1970s was to experiment with replacing the five-day, eight-hour week with a four-day, ten-hour week. This did not prove popular with most workers, however, and by the 1990s this approach had largely been abandoned, with a few exceptions. By 1985, about 15 percent of large corporations in the United States had adopted "flex-time" policies instead. Such a policy requires workers to conform to a core of common hours but allows them to change their hours outside of this core to accommodate personal and family needs, so long as they put in forty hours a week.

Most smaller businesses have yet to adopt flex-time practices. Brian Gill (1998) noted that the executives in these firms have overlooked the benefits of such scheduling, which he says include the reduction of short-term absences, tardiness , and morning coffee talk time. Also, employees are more likely to work during the most productive hours of the day and to be more job-focused; some businesses can use flex time to offer more service to customers who prefer early-morning or late-evening hours. Despite these benefits, many employees at small businesses today believe that they take flex time at the risk of their jobs.

Sociological practitioners in Europe (Brewster, Mayne, and Tegaskis 1997) surveyed the prevalence of flexible scheduling in work settings in fourteen European countries. They found that flexibility is widespread and growing, but their concept of flexibility includes part-time work and contract or nonpermanent employment—what we call temp jobs in the United States—as well as flexible hours. They also found that all of the forms of flexibility offer some advantages to employees who must fit household and family obligations and activities into an often-rigid framework in standard work settings. From another perspective, the changes rapidly taking place across Europe are mainly advantageous to owners and managers who seek to increase labor cost efficiencies. Workers often must settle for lower pay or reduced benefits, both of which have significant ramifications for their ownership and consumer patterns. The social and economic orders, the authors argue, are generally based on standard job terms, even though substantial numbers of households are not organized around such a standard any more.

OCCUPATIONAL MOBILITY

Sociologists have always placed great importance on upward and downward occupational mobility within industrial societies. In a fluid, competitive society, the prospect for workers to move up in position, and thus in monetary rewards, has been a central theme of capitalist economies. This type of mobility differs from that of movement up or down in income and other resources by *whole* occupational categories and social classes.

In a calm economy, workers in secure jobs can expect that, to some extent, mobility will be tied to competence and performance; that demotions will happen to the most incompetent, poorest performers; and that promotions and raises (at least part of the time, chance and unfairness aside) will be given to the most deserving workers. In this kind of bell curve of performance qualities, of course, most employees would reach a kind of plateau, particularly in static firms where there are far fewer positions at the top than at the bottom or in the middle.

Under the onslaught of computerization, globalization, and the adjustive actions of downsizing, reorganizing, and the like, worker mobility prospects often become too uncertain to be predicted with any accuracy. Positions may be eliminated, consolidated, or transferred to another location within a few weeks. Tasks may be redefined and redistributed so that a competent worker gets reassigned to a set of tasks that requires less skill, and thus is put at risk because she is overqualified for the new job. In the absence of union protection, the same job may be assigned a lower wage after the firm is restructured, or a worker may keep his wage level yet be assigned to far less challenging types of work. The formerly unusual event of being demoted and getting a lower wage is now an everpresent danger.

When upward mobility is blocked for individuals and a stratum of workers regionally or nationally is experiencing no improvement in life prospects, the job dissatisfactions explored earlier are seriously intensified. Turnover rates go up; hostility and cynicism often become epidemic within a work force; and, for many employees, the old incentives for a high level of effort are eliminated, generating a downward spiral of work performance. These conditions became widespread within the U.S. Postal Service (USPS) in the 1990s, for example. So many instances of conflict, disruption, and breakdown took place that the phrase "going postal" became a part of the national vocabulary (referring to a violent form of acting-out of hostility).

The USPS is the world's largest materials-handling operation. It employs nearly 745,000 workers and functions through 40,000 post offices and substations. About 43,000 workers were laid off in 1991, and 10,000 in 1992, with tens of thousands of additional layoffs projected for subsequent years. U.S. Postmaster General Anthony M. Frank, a banker, undertook a drive to automate the Service and to make it conform to a business rather than a public-service model of operations (Cook 1992). As private companies such as Federal Express and the United Parcel Service began to cut into the USPS's market share in the 1980s, and as postal rates failed to keep pace with demands on the delivery system, the level of service by the USPS began to fall. Deliveries were curtailed, collections were reduced, and customer complaints soared. Frank also privatized sectors of the Service and introduced what he called "work sharing," so that selected customer groups could get discounts by doing part of the work of preparing bulk mailings. He introduced as many other labor cost-cutting practices as the union contract would permit.

In short, Frank revamped the Postal Service from top to bottom after it had suffered a decade of confusion, turmoil, and both intramural and service failures. One in every ten Postal Service employees was laid off; others were reassigned to new tasks; daily work operations were radically redesigned; and severely protracted negotiations and arbitration over a labor contract poisoned the USPS well for employees generally. The USPS became a kind of microcosm of all of the pathologies that come into play in work settings when too much change is introduced too fast and under conditions that are patently unfavorable to the stability and mobility prospects of employees. Those pathologies, in a concentrated form, repeatedly triggered acts of rage, revenge, and homicidal and suicidal endangerment among workers and former employees.

CONCLUSION

Sociological practice within the field of business, industrial, and labor relations has been part of the discipline for a century. This chapter has emphasized the jagged line that must be drawn, however, between practice in the industrial period (1900–1960) and practice today. The latter period is one of computerization, globalization, and corresponding transformations in the nature of work and the conditions of employment. These are taking place at such uneven rates and in so many varied ways around the world that valid generalizations are difficult to make. We are in a period of swift and radical reorganization of production, distribution, and service exchange operations worldwide.

The profiles of work being done by sociologists Arthur Shostak and Richard Kronish show that long-established patterns of technical assistance by sociologists to labor unions persist even as unions themselves, at least in the United States, continue to shrink in scale and potency. There could be a resurgence of organized labor, to be sure, if new sources of member participation and new incentives for organizing can be found, but the current economic period is too turbulent to make accurate forecasting possible.

Sociologists who do enter the field of business and industrial relations do so, for the most part, through the doors of human resources and training and development departments of large corporations. A few are employed by research and development consulting firms who service labor union headquarters in the national capitals of Western countries. Others come in through service in the U.S. Department of Labor and its Bureau of Labor Statistics and counterpart agencies in European governments. However, the numbers of practitioners in these agencies are small and most of the work is carried out by labor economists.

REFERENCES

Abrama, L., et al. August 1997. The institutionalization of the sociology of work in Latin America. *Work and Occupations* 24, no. 3: 348–64.

Braverman, H. 1974. *Labor and Monopoly Capital.* New York: Monthly Review.

Brewster, C., L. Mayne, and O. Tegaskis. Summer 1997. Flexible working in Europe. *Journal of World Business* 32, no. 2: 133–52.

Burack, E. H., and R. P. Singh. March 1995. The new employment relations compact. *Human Resources Planning* 18, no. 1: 13.

Burris, B. H. 1998. Computerization in the workplace. *Annual Review of Sociology* 22, no. 1: 141–58.

Byrne, J. A. 1994. The pain of downsizing. *Business Week*, 9 May, 60–69.

Cook, J. 1992. A mailman's lot is not a happy one. *Forbes* 149, no. 9: 82–89.

Dutton, G. September 1998. Cutting-edge stressbusters. *HR Focus* 75, no. 9: 11–13.

Erickson, C. L., and S. Kuruvilla. October 1998. Industrial relations system transformation. *Industrial and Labor Relations Review* 52, no. 1: 3–22.

Ettore, B. August 1993. Will unions survive? *Management Review* 82, no. 8: 9–16.

Ezzy, D. August 1997. Subjectivity and the labour process: Conceptualizing "Good Work." *Sociology* 31, no. 3: 427–45.

Geoghegan, T. 1992. Confessions of a labor lawyer. *Across the Board* 29, nos. 1–2: 12.

Gill, B. February 1998. Flextime benefits employees and employers. *American Printer* 220, no. 5: 70.

Hackett, R. D., and P. Bycio. December 1996. An evaluation of employee absenteeism as a coping mechanism among hospital nurses. *Journal of Occupational and Organizational Psychology* 69, no. 4: 327–39.

Modic, S. J. 1987. How's your quality of work life? *Industry Week.* 233 (June 15): 7.

Paquet, R., and J. Bergeron. Spring 1996. An explanatory model of participation in union activity. *Labor Studies Journal* 21, no. 1: 3.

Rothman, R. A. 1987. *Working: Sociological Perspectives.* Englewood Cliffs, N.J.: Prentice Hall.

Shostak, A. B. 1999. *CyberUnion: Empowering Labor through Technology.* Philadelphia: M.E. Sharpe.

Whyte, W. F., and J. R. Blasi. 1984. Union ownership and the future. *Annals of the American Academy of Political and Social Science* 476: 128–40.
Yates, M. D. February 1997. Does labor have a future? *Monthly Review* 48, no. 9: 1–18.

5

Education

INTRODUCTION

The institution of education in the Western world is as old as Greek antiquity. Greek city-states maintained academies within which youth were taught the arts and sciences of the times and prepared both physically and mentally for leadership roles in the society and economy of their generation. Sociologist Emile Durkheim founded the modern concept of education as the transmission of culture in his writings on the institution at the turn of the nineteenth century (Durkheim 1956).

It is the postindustrial, postmodern era of the second half of the twentieth century that has transformed education. The institution, at all levels from preschool through graduate professional schools, has increased greatly in importance even while it has declined in clarity. Enlargement of participation in schooling in the United States began to accelerate immediately after World War II. The G.I. Bill, which paid for schooling for millions of war veterans, multiplied tremendously the scale of enrollment in both colleges and vocational-technical schools. Concurrently, high school enrollments swelled as youths who previously would have gone directly from grade 8 or 9 into the work force now continued into high school. With the advent of the Baby Boom, elementary and secondary school facilities had to be expanded enormously between 1950 and 1970.

Two kinds of forces impelled this growth. First, technology was changing rapidly in scope and complexity, requiring a more highly educated work force to operate and control it. This included electronic communications, air transport, and new modes of manufacturing, for example. Second, the central societal question concerning schooling has long been that of who shall be educated. When economic production was fueled principally by the availability of abundant unskilled labor, education was of importance primarily to the upper classes and to those seeking to enter the learned professions and scientific or technical occupations. As recently as 1940 in the United States, and in most nations of the West, only about one-third of each generation's youths attended high school and even fewer graduated. By 1955, that proportion had expanded to three-fourths. The enlargement of education also affected systems other than schools: government and industry created training systems that together were larger than all of public schooling combined; radio, recording, television, and later the Internet provided educational alternatives that were vast in both scope and capabilities.

As educational involvement expands, its nature and operations become less understandable. Public assumptions about what is entailed do not keep pace with changes in the institution; at the same time, cultural and technological changes occur so swiftly that the institution often lags far behind the imperatives cross-pressuring it to modernize and adapt. This increasing lack of clarity, as well as frustrations generated by the change process, have made education a fertile field for social scientific analysis and for applied contributions to its redesign or articulation in line with the needs of the time.

SOME OF THE MILESTONES

In the years from 1910 to 1930, a subgroup of sociologists who called themselves educational sociologists emerged. They worked in government agencies, school districts, college and university administrations, but above all in departments of social foundations that had been established in normal schools for teachers and then state teachers' colleges and eventually in land-grant universities. These departments brought together professors of philosophy, history, sociology, economics, government, and anthropology. The great American philosopher John Dewey was such a professor. Foundations' faculty often collaborated closely with faculty in social studies, where they helped to shape curricula in high school and junior high school history and geography.

The educational sociologists never became heroes in the annals of academic sociology because they practiced their profession as opposed to building the academic discipline. Their mission was to use the knowledge of their field in educational administration and planning and to help prepare teachers by providing knowledge about the family, community, religion, and other contextual institutions. They go unsung because they stepped out of the mainstream of the American Sociological Association; because they did not seek to build a science of sociology; and because they partook of the moral zeal inherent in the culture of schoolteachers everywhere. This zeal did not appear to academic sociologists to fit neatly into the cool, dry distance they regarded as appropriate to scientific inquiry as the field came into the 1950s.

They also get overlooked in the history of the profession of education itself because that profession has been dominated by psychologists and psychological theories and research for a century. Schools of education and training-system managers alike draw most heavily from the ranks of psychologists. The American Psychological Association and most large faculty departments of psychology include specialists in learning theory, child and adolescent development, educational psychology and psychometrics, counseling and clinical psychology, and cognitive psychology, for example, and each of these specialties in turn provides conceptual and empirical resources to branches of professional education. There are at least twenty psychologists who focus on education, in one sector or another, for every one sociologist of education.

In the 1930s, a sociology of education emerged from the work of the Committee on Human Development within the School of Education at the University of Chicago. The work of William Lloyd Warner (Warner and Havighurst 1945), Allison Davis (1947), and later Robert Havighurst, among others, showed how sociological inquiry could have substantial practical utility for education. They broke through the boundaries between the disciplines of psychology, anthropology, and sociology, and collaborated very fruitfully with educators. These sociologists built on the philosophical thought of John Dewey, William Cooley, W. E. B. DuBois, and Lester Ward. The Committee became a world-class center for thought, empirical inquiry, and practical experimentation in education.

New York University's School of Education put similar importance on applied social research in that period. There, public school teachers and administrators became applied sociologists and vice versa, as the quest for solutions to educational problems became increasingly scientific. Dan Dodson was one of the leaders of this group. He catalogued and described many of the practical consequences of the applications of that time (Dodson 1952). Just six years later, Orville G. Brim (1958) opened the current era of the sociology of education, just as the door to educational sociology was closing.

Sociologists at Johns Hopkins University, under initiatives begun by James S. Coleman, Peter H. Rossi, Edward L. McDill, and James McPartland, created a research and development center called the Center for the Study of School Organization, which worked in the mid-1960s on kindergarten-through-grade-12 educational questions. Over the past thirty-five years, the name of the center has changed repeatedly as different requirements were imposed by contracts with the U.S. Department of Education, but the mission has remained very constant. The Center focuses on solutions to inequality of educational opportunity among racial and ethnic groups in the United States, and on organizational and curricular strategies for remedying those inequalities and closing the achievement gap between ethnic minorities and white students and between low-income and higher-income students. As a result of close collaboration between the Center and the Johns Hopkins Department of Sociology, a cadre of sociologists have earned their Ph.D.s by doing research and development work at the Center.

The career of Dr. Lee G. Burchinal also exemplifies the tradition of involvement in education by American sociologists. Burchinal joined the department of sociology at Iowa State University in 1956 as a traditional academician and teacher. In 1962, he accepted a position with a federal social research program and became a grants manager. With the advent of the War on Poverty in 1964, Burchinal became deputy director of the Division of Research in the U.S. Office of Education (the precursor to the current Department of Education).

The Division was operating a small, unfunded unit called the Educational Research Information Center (ERIC). It functioned as a kind of clearinghouse and knowledge repository for researchers and practitioners. Burchinal took charge of ERIC and built it into one of the world's most authoritative, computer-based, knowledge-exchange services in the world. He rejected the model of a centralized bureaucracy within the government. Instead, he opted for a decentralized system based on subject-oriented clearinghouses run by professionals in their own settings at universities and professional associations. To this system he added private firms to assist with operating ERIC.

Today, ERIC has evolved into an information system that has set the pattern for a wide range of such systems operated through the Internet and through university libraries and other large libraries worldwide. Documents based on research and development projects are stored electronically. Abstracts are coded so that they lead users to storehouses for microfiche and microfilm collections of the documents. The system incorporates many reports from teachers, school administrators, and other clinical practitioners as well. Its system properties have evolved in tandem with the changing technology of computers; however, the underlying design by Lee Burchinal, which was fundamentally sociological in its reliance on existing professional networks and a wide-ranging, flexible set of contributing sources, has remained quite stable.

Education became a major domain for sociological practitioners in the years from 1960 through 1975. During this period, educational change and improvement increasingly became linked to the civil rights movement, student protest and reform movements within the countercultures of the era, and both economic development and liberation theology movements in Latin America and other parts of what was then defined as the Third World. The search for ways to adapt schools and college to meet the changing needs of children, youth, and adult learners, and to improve the efficacy of educational activities, elicited great enthusiasm among applied sociologists.

Indeed, it was in this same fertile period that American sociology began to become self-aware and reflexive. Its often stiflingly dull introductory courses were revisited and revised; the American Sociological Association, with leadership from Dr. Hans Mauksch, who had pioneered in bringing sociology into the curricula of schools of nursing in America, began to assist in developing excellent instructional materials and in sponsoring a good journal on *Teaching Sociology*. Better textbooks and novel laboratory materials and research exercises sprang into being in these years.

The bloom on the tree of sociological practice in education began to fade after 1975. Students majoring in elementary and secondary education declined greatly in numbers. New occupational opportunities for women in business and the professions had a strongly negative effect on enrollments in schools of education where, historically, women had constituted three-quarters to four-fifths of the student bodies. Several hundred of the nation's 1,300 schools and departments of education were disestablished in the decade after 1975. With the end of the Baby Boom, moreover, the reduction of school enrollments affected opportunities in the field, as the new wave of women elected to have no children or just one or two at most, in contrast to their mothers. Openings for beginning teachers approached zero in most states; only California, Florida, Texas, and one or two other sunbelt states were hiring any beginners. As a result, positions in the social sciences that depended on continuous expansion of the field were cut back severely, and by the advent of the Reagan administration in the early 1980s, federal funding for educational projects plummeted. Funding for educational services has since been increased in many states, but federal investments have gone increasingly to the states. The funding and infrastructure of universities, colleges, research and development groups, and support centers for planning and technical assistance—the locations where many applied sociologists of education were based—were never restored.

PERSISTING THEMES

Applied sociologists have made significant contributions to educational research, development, and practice because the fit between the prevailing content of sociology and the practice of formal education is strategically ideal. Education takes place within the context of society; thus, it is directly and intimately affected by the social structure; by class, racial, and ethnic patterns; by the intersecting institutions of family and community; and by the age and gender groups of both students and teachers. As globalization takes place and societies modernize within it, moreover, cross-national comparisons of educational subsystems become a natural part of the sociological enterprise.

Secondly, schooling is a social institution in its own right. It is a web of agencies and professional associations. It is also a major labor force and a part of the postindustrial world in which occupational placement, mobility, career paths, and unions affect the performance of social tasks.

The fit between education and sociology is close for a third reason. There is a micro-sociology that is suited to analysis of the ethnography of classrooms, the symbolic interaction processes of school staffs and students, and the sociometric analysis of peer groupings. As part of this field, sociologists have worked hard to develop models of how knowledge and new ideas are diffused and exchanged.

A fourth sector of activity has been the study and evaluation of educational activities outside of schools. Studies and development work on media influence, the design of training programs in government and industry, and more recently the emergence of educational programming as part of distance learning through the Internet are part of what applied sociologists do. For sociologists, education has always been a socialization process that includes but also transcends schooling.

SOCIETY AND EDUCATION

From within the sociological perspective, the institution of education is little more than a spot on the tail of the societal dog. Its structure and functions are refracted versions of the social order and its processes. Educators inhabit a societal context in which some work to prepare students for a changing future, while some others on the opposite end of the spectrum work to transmit a culture that in part is locked into a series of outmoded ideas and fact patterns. Most, however, work within the frame of current societal constructs and tend to reproduce the prevailing status quo.

In preindustrial societies, education is merged with the practices of other social groups: the tribal community, clan, feudal estate, and family. As a society industrializes, education follows the trend in all other institutions and becomes more and more markedly differentiated as a distinctive enterprise in itself. As this process matures, moreover, the importance of education increases. This condition can be reversed, at least temporarily. When the Shah of Iran secularized and sought to modernize the state in 1936, for example, he eliminated the mandate that all females wear the veil (a symbol of piety, modesty, and subordination). As millions of women threw off their veils, education was simultaneously extended to include Iranian girls and women. With the advent of the Islamic Revolution of 1978, however, the veil requirement was reinstated and the old restrictions of educational opportunities were renewed. Generally, however, industrialization and modernization generate conditions for increasing inclusiveness and universality of educational opportunities. Sociological practitioners have worked to facilitate this growth for racial and ethnic minorities, women, socioeconomically deprived groups, and today, gay and lesbian students. Within the framework of this growth, the ranks of practitioners themselves have changed dramatically since 1960, becoming ever more representative of the makeup of the population at large.

As demographic and technological changes sweep across the world in this postmodern era, adaptations in education are rarely if ever objectively self-evident. Each adaptation (and each decision not to adapt) requires a social scientific foundation of evidence and a set of cultural constructs that interpret the ways in which to adapt. After World War II, for instance, the United States demobilized many millions of conscripted military men and women. How to reintegrate them into the society became a major policy question. One of the resulting answers was the G.I. Bill, which was intended to fund education and housing for the returnees. Existing schools, colleges, and universities were not designed to host these veterans and initial trepidations were strong, as was the belief among many educators that most of the veterans would not be capable of undertaking higher learning. Within one year, however, these concerns were laid to rest as hundreds of thousands of men and women poured into the schools and flourished academically. So great was the impact, in fact, that this is often marked as the threshold of a great widening of educational opportunity—from an opportunity formerly reserved for the wealthy and the gifted, to one shared by youth and young adults from all parts of U.S. society. In contrast, the women who had replaced men in the work force were not retained, and had to retreat from the jobs they had performed so well back into sex-segregated occupations and the role of housewife. Both of these profound changes are the result of vast demographic shifts and of changing cultural interpretations of how those shifts should be viewed.

FAMILIES AND EDUCATION

Sociologists have been instrumental in illuminating the connections between family life and school learning. For example, the great French sociologist Phillipe Aries (1962) was among the first to show, through historical analysis, how the very concept of childhood had been transformed by the advent of industrialization and urbanization. Children as we now define them did not emerge until late in the eighteenth century, and family units were very different in structures and functions in earlier days.

Families and the religious groups to which they belonged took care of educating the young, save for members of the aristocracy and members of the priesthood, until the time of the aftermath of the French Revolution. Schooling was a late development for the masses of children, and schools themselves stressed piety and obedience rather than cognitive mastery of skills and subject matter. Traditional, institutional families, in contrast to the more individualistic, companionate, and nuclear families of this century, were in charge of educating the young. As schooling became more universal and then compulsory, family control over the scope, content, and extent of schooling continued to shape the educational experiences of all children.

Even as family control diminishes, however, the early effects of the household as a carrier of socioeconomic status and the subcultural orientations built into social status have changed very little. Middle- and upper-status households tend to socialize infants and preschoolers toward preparation for the role of student in a school. Reading, conversation, and cognitive challenges are often part of the contextual fabric of these homes, whereas they are absent as resources for very young children in homes at or below the poverty line. There is more to this family effect than status, moreover: there is training in aspiration, in goal setting, and in competitive disposition toward achievement. In these respects and others, the higher status child arrives at the schoolhouse door—especially if he or she is white and English-speaking—knowing what is expected, able to meet the student role requirements, and practiced in aspiring to achieve cognitively and socially.

Sociologists have labored for nearly a century documenting this proposition and pointing out various practical implications in it for improving the learning opportunities of all children. Ironically, many of the instructional, curricular, and student support ideas that have been tested since the 1960s entail challenges to conventional parental attitudes (Levine and Havighurst 1992, 100–102) and thus play up conflicts between subsets of families and the more innovative community schools.

PEER INFLUENCES

As family control over the lives of children has declined, and as families have ceded much of their control over socialization to other institutions, including schools (Ianni 1989; Kamarck and Galston 1990), peer influences have increased steadily in recent decades. Part of this is a mechanical function of the fact that most schools are very age-graded and thus create settings that are mediated by groups of age mates. Children and youth in Western societies spend less and less time with their parents in any event, less time with their teachers as they mature into adolescence, and ever more time in peer groups.

The challenge for educators is to find ways to help shape peer relationships into a positive developmental force in the lives of learners. Robert Slavin (1991) and applied sociologists at Johns Hopkins University have pioneered in designing and field-testing school projects in which students join in cooperative teams guided by trained staff to share work on learning problems. The Slavin projects begin in elementary school and extend upward through the grades. They teach interpersonal and small-group skills, encourage cooperation and mutual social support rather than aggressive competition, and create "prosocial" learning situations.

Recent studies of middle-class black students who perform poorly on achievement tests in middle and high school further illuminate the power of the peer group effect (Belluck 1999). The National Task Force on Minority High School Achievement, formed in 1997 by the College Board, analyzed nationwide 1995 SAT scores and found that all races had better scores if the parents had more education, but that blacks whose parents had at least one graduate degree averaged 191 points lower than whites whose parents had the same amount of education. Interviews with high school students in several affluent suburban high schools revealed not only that many black students experience social and competitive discomfort in racially mixed student groups, but also that some black peer reactions are hostile toward high achievement. One highly motivated black high school junior explained, black "[p]eople were like, 'Oh, you're an oreo.' Getting good grades was always connected to white people. So they're like, 'Are you going to be white and achieve?'"

As contemporary adolescents increasingly detach from their families and hew more closely to peer groups, most high schools today are fragmented into subcultures of social cliques, which play a powerful role in shaping the social climate of each school (Coleman 1961). The Columbine High School tragedy, in which two students killed and wounded a teacher and thirteen students in April, 1999, had at its base a clique of boys who were visibly and actively alienated from the mainstream of the school. Within the clique. two boys were committed nihilistically to lethal hostility toward other groups of students, particularly student athletes. Less deadly examples are available daily from nearly every high school in America. Finding ways to identify progressively alienated peer groups and developing ways to prevent further erosion of intergroup relations is a leading challenge facing future sociological practitioners.

THE EXAMPLE OF RACIAL AND ETHNIC MINORITIES

In the United States, no subgroup of the population has been more systematically excluded from educational opportunity than African Americans.

This exclusion, built into state laws since the days of slavery, had the sanction of the Constitution and federal policy behind it from the formation of the Union until the 1954 Supreme Court decision in *Brown v Topeka Board of Education*. Exclusion was initially strategic. Prohibition of literacy for slaves helped to ensure the inability of African Americans to develop a broad-based movement of revolution and to demonstrate the scope of white supremacy. After emancipation, the effort to eliminate exclusion was short-lived, as separate and egregiously inferior schools and colleges for African Americans were established throughout all of the former slave states and in many other states as well.

W. E. B. DuBois (1968), Charles Johnson (Robbins 1997), Allison Davis (1947), and Franklin Frazier (1951) were among the many African American sociologists who worked diligently in the decades before the *Brown* decision to achieve educational equality for racial minorities. In their era, racially separated, segregated schooling was explicit and, in thirteen states, a matter of law. They concentrated their efforts, for these reasons, on the quest for improved schooling for Negroes (later called blacks and, later still, African Americans). The gaps they identified and struggled to close were extreme: Negro teachers were paid less than half the going wage for white teachers; facilities, equipment, and materials were almost uniformly deplorable, outdated, and in poor repair. The entire contrast expressed, in every observable way to anyone who noticed, the vast inferiority in treatment of Negroes. The gap in achievement scores was such that Negro students in grade 10, for instance, averaged half the percentile score of whites.

After the *Brown* decision, which held that racially separate schooling was unconstitutional, political resistance to change was so intense that little was accomplished toward desegregating schools or equalizing treatment between 1955 and 1965. A few districts in such border states as Maryland and in the District of Columbia complied with little fanfare; in the North, New York and Massachusetts began to establish policies that fostered desegregation. After passage of the Civil Rights Act by Congress in 1964, however, change began to take hold in hundreds of racially mixed school districts, most often under federal court orders but in some instances by action of the U.S. Department of Justice and the Office of Education.

Sociological practitioners were very pertinent to progress in eliminating school segregation in the 1960–1985 time span. At the University of California at Berkeley, the University of Chicago, the University of Illinois at Chicago Circle, New York University, Columbia Teachers College, the R&D

Center at Johns Hopkins, and the Center for Urban Education in New York City, sociologists demonstrated that they had the methodological and problem-solving tools appropriate to working on this form of racial inequality. They made comparative analyses of schools and programs for the two major racial groups; researched the scope and extent, as well as the housing and organizational sources, of segregative policies; helped to measure and define the nature of district liability for wrongs done to racial minorities; and, above all, contributed greatly to the formulation, planning, and implementation of remedies and alternative, more equalized practices. They also engaged in research evaluations of the impact and effectiveness of various remedies. Other sociologists, including Garth Taylor (1978), did surveys of public acceptance of desegregative changes.

The bearing of sociology on school desegregation was grounded in a long period of sociologists' intellectual work on race relations on the one hand and the evolution of the sociology of education on the other. Student and teacher assignment patterns were part of public school enrollment patterns and were ideally suited to demographic analysis, projections, and the identification of alternatives. Locating new school facilities within communities so as to foster racial integration between residential neighborhoods was part of the tool kit of community analysis common to sociology.

Sociologist James S. Coleman was commissioned in 1964 by the U.S. Office of Education, under a mandate from the U.S. Congress, to research the extent nationwide of racial segregation and to measure its effects on students. The result (Coleman et al. 1966) was one of the largest studies ever conducted on schools—or, indeed, on any social institution. His findings documented the facts of segregation and its pervasiveness, but also showed that the effects of schooling on student achievement were associated much more substantially with family background variables, especially those of socioeconomic status, and with peer influences than with race or schooling itself. Coleman and his colleagues concluded that if a student was a Negro, came from a working-class family, and attended a public school that was very predominantly composed of working-class peers, he or she would have, on average, low academic achievement scores. Subsequent studies by Wilson (1967), Orland (1990), and Mosteller and Moynihan (1972) supported this finding. The policy implication was that school outcomes are shaped primarily by family background and the peer mix (both racial and socioeconomic), of students in a school.

A social issue as complex and vast as race and education could not be expected to enlist sociologists on only one side of the question. David Armor and Nathan Glazer were just two of the sociologists who opposed school desegregation as early as the beginning of the 1970s, for instance. Armor, located for much of his career at the Rand Corporation in Santa Monica, California, a leading social research and planning firm, devoted his energies for a quarter of a century to criticizing desegregation plans; attacking cross-neighborhood busing of students in particular; elaborating on the threat of "white flight" (the withdrawal of white households from city schools); and, later, to guiding school districts on ways to terminate federal court jurisdiction over schools. Practicing sociologists increasingly were retained as expert witnesses and planners, both by those who advocated desegregation and by those who opposed it strenuously. Although most were enlisted by advocates of civil rights and educational change, opponents had more resources to invest and often spent it on sociologists such as Armor. Other sociologists, including James Coleman himself, supported one side of the policy dispute and later changed their minds. Coleman had supported school integration during the 1960s. He came to regard the change process as too conflictual to be desirable, however, and began to oppose the mandatory reassignment of students in the 1970s. In 1975, he became the first sociologist ever to give an address to the legislature of Massachusetts, warning against desegregation of the schools of Boston and the dangers of white flight.

My own career work on racial desegregation of public schools, colleges, and universities typifies the ways in which practicing sociologists engaged this facet of American education. As a sociologist of urban education at Teachers College, Columbia University, I was appointed director of the college's new Institute of Urban Studies in 1963. The New York State Commissioner of Education, James Allen, appointed John Fischer, then president of Teachers College and previously superintendent of the Baltimore, Maryland, public schools; Kenneth Clark, professor of psychology at City College of New York; and Rabbi Judah Kahn to recommend ways to desegregate the public schools of New York City in 1963. With my leading sociology doctoral student, Richard Boardman, I became the staff for this commission's planning project. Fischer had overseen the desegregation of Baltimore schools and Clark had been a major expert witness in the *Brown* case before the Supreme Court. All three had done smaller projects for Allen earlier.

Desegregation in New York City schools could have been accomplished at that time. The commission trio and Boardman and I, in *Desegregating the Public Schools of New York City* (Fischer et al. 1964), recommended actions the City Board of Education could take, with state assistance, toward this end. Siting intermediate schools of grades 6–8 on the boundaries of racial ghettoes was one of the recommendations that was not only adopted but also implemented, leading to the transformation of junior high schools into the middle schools of the future. The technique of clustering schools and pairing them to foster cross-race assignments of pupils from black and white neighborhoods was described and outlined. A dozen other desegregative strategies were also presented. These were endorsed by Commissioner Allen and the New York Board of Regents and were given endorsement "in principle" by the City Board of Education—but, as sociologist David Rogers reported a few years later (1969) in his study of the city system, the actions were never carried out.

I became director of the Center for Urban Education, a federally funded regional education laboratory, in 1965. The Center, under my direction, was very actively involved in planning the racial desegregation of schools in White Plains, Rochester, and Buffalo, New York; Bridgeport and Stamford, Connecticut; and a host of other smaller districts in the greater New York metropolitan region. Other sociologists joined me and Boardman in this work, including Max Wolff, Mary Ellen Warshauer, Gladys Lang, Herbert Gans, and Jerald Handel.

Work in progress by this group flourished under the administration of Lyndon Johnson and its "Great Society" campaign. Desegregation plans were linked explicitly to ways of improving the quality of educational services provided to black and other minority children. By the middle of Richard Nixon's first term, however, federal support for any kind of school desegregation languished, and the Center fell into political disfavor.

As a result, I relocated to Boston from New York City and began to serve as Dean of Education at Boston University. Federal District Judge W. Arthur Garrity called on me in January 1975 to ask my help in planning the desegregation of the public schools of Boston. As a court-appointed expert, I worked initially under the leadership of a panel of four court masters, one of whom was sociologist Charles V. Willie from the Harvard Graduate School of Education. With my associate Marvin B. Scott and the masters, we formulated a plan for Boston, which was needed because proposals submitted by the Boston school authorities proved unacceptable to the court.

There is great hesitancy within courts about intruding into local educational affairs. Courts are not good settings in which to resolve educational disputes, which are best dealt with by state and local authorities and by co-participation with federal agencies when national civil rights standards are in question. Thus, the tradition since the *Brown* decision in 1954 was that school boards and state boards of education were obligated, even when convicted of intentional segregation, to devise alternatives to current practice. Attorneys for black plaintiffs also seldom involved themselves in educational planning, at least before approaches began to shift in the 1980s. Therefore, Judge Garrity, recognizing that he could not expect to receive a constitutionally sound plan from the Boston authorities, elicited proposals from all of the parties in the suit, and our team began to piece elements from each of them into a single, unified plan.

The court masters retired from the case after six weeks of service. Judge Garrity asked Scott and me to stay on, however, to help him make small revisions in the draft plan and, later, to serve as his liaison between the courthouse and the Boston School Department. Scott served from 1975 to 1984, and I continued to serve from 1975 until 1990.

We told our story in a book, *Schools on Trial: An Inside Account of the Boston Desegregation Case* (Dentler and Scott 1981). The application of sociology was pivotal: it made possible the analysis of enrollments, differentiated between the residential subcommunities within the city, enabled the convening of leadership groups for planning, and laid a basis for monitoring compliance with each facet of the court orders. This was all carried out under conditions of substantial social and political stress. Judge Garrity was vilified and under constant threat, as well as round-the-clock security by U.S. Marshals and the F.B.I. He drew most of the direct fire in the racial conflicts that flared repeatedly in 1974 through 1977.

I went on to work on similar court cases in St. Louis, Missouri; Little Rock, Arkansas; Kansas City, Missouri; Mobile, Alabama; and Rockford, Illinois. I also served as a chief witness for the U.S. Office of Civil Rights in a large suit against the University of North Carolina, and co-authored a book on that case (Dentler, Baltzell, and Sullivan 1983). In the mid-1980s I served in a similar capacity in the litigation of *United States v. Alabama*, the prosecution of the University of Alabama system for segregation.

By the late 1980s, the U.S. Supreme Court had undertaken a persistent assault on the opinions of the earlier era that had led to both desegregation and affirmative action policies of many kinds. By the late 1990s, most of the nation's progress toward equal educational treatment during the 1960s and 1970s had been reversed. Desegregation policies were dismantled and civil rights attorneys began to abandon efforts to prevent deep and wide setbacks in what they had accomplished earlier. The sociologist who utilizes his or her knowledge and skills in the service of a social cause, even one as profound as the cause of the civil rights movement, should expect to witness a process of pendular swings toward justice followed by reversions to an earlier status quo.

A different illustration of sociological practice in school desegregation comes from the work of Charles V. Willie and Michael Alves in their invention and implementation of Controlled Choice plans (Willie, Alves, and Hagerty 1996). Controlled Choice is a method of achieving school desegregation that these sociologists first implemented in the public schools of Cambridge, Massachusetts, in 1981. Since then, several school districts in Massachusetts have adopted versions of Controlled Choice, and a handful of districts from Florida to California have followed suit.

The central idea in Controlled Choice is that parents of students choose which schools they would most like their children to attend, within a large subdistrict zone of a city or the total district in the case of a smaller district. Student populations are designed, based on the parental choice preferences, to have the same proportions by race and ethnicity as those in the zones or the total district, within a range of allowable variance. Priority of assignment is given to siblings and to students who can walk to schools near their homes; however, walk-zone students, as they are called, get priority according to the racial fairness guidelines described earlier. Parents are asked to rank three choices, from first to third. The choice data become a reference on the relative attractiveness of schools, and school boards using Controlled Choice are supposed to give special attention to the least chosen schools, which are presumed to be in need of improvement.

The most recent application of Controlled Choice took place in the Rockford, Illinois, public schools, under the aegis of a federal court that sought a remedy for intentional and systematic racial segregation. A report on the effectiveness and public acceptance of the plan was published in 1999, based on the first two years of implementation (Taylor and Alves 1999). Almost 100 percent of all ninth-grade students and about 90 percent of all seventh-grade students were assigned to their parents' first choices as of the 1998 assignment process, and about 77 percent of kindergarten students also got their first choices. The survey of participating parents showed very high, widespread acceptance of the plan, even though most school board members continued their highly vocal disapproval of the plan and its results and called for a return to neighborhood (i.e., racially segregated) schools.

EDUCATIONAL DISADVANTAGEMENT

Schooling takes places within a social institution imbedded in the larger society. Its goals, design, and beneficiaries all reflect the ways in which advantages are distributed and controlled by groups in that larger society. Free public education has been far from universally available in American society throughout the twentieth century. Only one-third of the nation's public school students went beyond an eighth-grade education in 1940, for instance, and until the 1960s girls were far less likely than boys to go on to college after high school. These are simply illustrations of the many ways in which schooling is generally configured to parallel and thus reproduce the class, race, gender, and age structures of the society.

So, too, a highly capitalistic economy helps to shape schooling in ways that make it essentially competitive, reserving rewards for those who perform well in school and ignoring or down-rating those who fall below a statistical norm in the academic race. Middle- and upper-class students begin their schooling with a series of advantages that predispose them to be the winners in this race, alongside an occasional winner who comes up to join or beat them even though he or she began at the back of the pack.

Lower-status and ethnic and minority students come onto the elementary school learning field comparatively unequipped to play the academic achievement game. Because of their lack of community and family cultural preparation, as well as their relatively sparse preschool learning opportunities, they often cannot meet teachers' initial expectations. Their school performances therefore tend to decline as they age. Many of these students, moreover, are left out of the circle of social supports provided by the larger, white-dominated, middle-class community. Their families are also not situated politically to secure the help of school staff to advocate for and facilitate their school progress.

Their position at the bottom of the local community social system and their concentration in relatively poor communities tend to ensure that their poverty, family vulnerabilities, and language differences translate over time within the school system into substantial educational disadvantage. Sociologist Caroline Persell characterized these conditions as "the process effect of structural dominance" (1977). She showed how, in the absence of deliberate policy commitments to offset the effect, nearly all forces within a local school district work together to translate high socioeconomic and ethnic status into high educational achievement. In a competitive environment, arrangements and resources aimed at meeting the needs of low-status groups get sacrificed.

Fairly massive investments began to be made by the federal government in 1964 to counterbalance the grossly unjust pattern of structural dominance. At the onset of the War on Poverty, and after passage of the Civil Rights Act, Congress passed and President Johnson signed the Elementary and Secondary Education Act (ESEA), which, among other investments, funneled billions of dollars into state and local school districts in the form of grants for compensatory education. The idea was that federal dollars were to be used to enhance and reinforce the learning opportunities of socioeconomically disadvantaged children and youth, through programs designed by local educators and coordinated by state authorities. ESEA funding persisted from 1964 through the 1990s. Although the investments have continued, their initial focus on the children of the poor has been blurred as state and local programs have been granted authority to use the funds in more diverse ways.

Compensatory programs have been evaluated repeatedly by both sociologists and educational researchers (for a review, see Levine and Havighurst 1992). Very early childhood programs such as Headstart have a proven efficacy, at least of a limited kind, on nutrition, health, and social competence, as well as a kind of "sleeper" effect of helping with academic achievement by the middle grades; therefore, they have been expanded in recent years by additional federal investments. Primary-grade compensatory programs have improved substantially since the 1970s and the evidence, much of it gained by sociologists participating in applied evaluations, suggests that most American public schools have upgraded their ability to teach mastery of basic academic skills to most students, including the children who enter school disadvantaged.

Generally, however, these compensatory benefits tend to decline as disadvantaged children enter grades seven through ten. Three factors contribute powerfully to this decline:

1. It is much harder to teach skills of critical thinking and creative problem solving than it is to teach the rudiments of reading and arithmetic.

2. Investments in improved instruction for disadvantaged students in these secondary grades have been slight over the decades.

3. Peer group influences opposing positive participation in school learning become more powerful each year at these grade levels.

In spite of hundreds of earnest experiments and reforms, American secondary schools remain, with terribly few exceptions, learning environments that favor students who arrive as high achievers and whose middle- and upper-income parents have the motivation, skill, and resources to support them in their efforts. Although the high school graduation rate has risen during the 1990s, and although college enrollment—especially at the community college level—has risen as well, the curriculum of all but a tiny fraction of public middle and high schools is designed to accommodate but *not* to raise the abilities of lower-income and minority students. What lingers is a policy question that looms far larger than schooling itself: Shall the nation become divided into an information economy and an economy that employs the technically and scientific illiterate? If the academic performance gap between educationally disadvantaged and advantaged adolescents is not closed, what other outcome might one expect?

SCHOOL VIOLENCE

Public concern for the safety of students and staff in schools reached its first peak in the early 1970s in the United States. A host of sociological studies confirmed the gravity of the problem of violence and the potential for increased violence within school settings (Foley 1990; Miller 1973). The general assumption guiding these studies and the plans recommended to improve safety was that the violence was linked to poverty, youth crime, and inner-city decay—and indeed, by far the most frequent incidents in the 1970s and 1980s took place within and around schools in these neighborhoods. The congressionally mandated Safe School Study Report, prepared by a team of social scientists within the U.S. Office of Education in 1978, found that more than one-third of robberies and assaults on youth occurred in urban public schools; that 5,000 teachers and other faculty were physically assaulted each month; and that about half a million students reported feeling afraid while at school.

The assumption about inner-city conditions alone was discarded in the late 1990s, when incidents of extreme violence erupted in schools in both rural and suburban settings. Headlines were filled with the names of such towns as Springfield, Oregon; West Paducah, Kentucky; Edinboro, Pennsylvania; Jonesboro, Arkansas; and Littleton, Colorado. These stunning tragedies made it plain that the sources of violence among children and youth included far more than urban poverty and gangs.

As with every other emergent social problem, the application of sociology depends primarily upon identification of a sound theory that could account for the sources of the problem. Nonsociological theories are also highly pertinent: schools need building security personnel, for instance, and physical and mechanical arrangements for preventing or reacting to a crisis. Counseling psychology and educational administration alike need greatly improved tools for identifying deep student alienation and rage and for countering these psychological conflicts early and effectively. Sociologists have collaborated with educators to develop training programs (Cardinale 1990) through which students learn how to mediate and resolve disputes without recourse to violence. Meanwhile, legislators and professionals within the justice system have focused on ways to enhance the controls available through law enforcement and to strengthen the means available for crisis management.

The key theories used by sociologists of education who work on the analysis and prevention of school violence, however, stem from the twin concepts of social organization and symbolic interaction. These include the concepts of social climates of schools (Coleman 1961), the sociometric structure, and related peer relations within classrooms (Hallinan and Teixeira 1987; Hallinan and Smith 1989; Hallinan and Williams 1990). The guiding notion (drawn from symbolic interactionism) is that the social organization of a school combines with its interpersonal environment of personal and intergroup relations to generate either conditions of social respect, trust, and acceptance, or conditions of disrespect, mistrust, rejection, and hostility. Empirical analysis of these conditions usually will not disclose the point at which alienation and hostility turn into murderous rage, but the latter, in the thinking of sociologists, very rarely arises in an environment that is accepting and inclusive.

OTHER SOURCES OF EDUCATION

As societies modernize, they invest increasingly greater resources in education. This institution becomes the vehicle for sorting and positioning young adults in the society and for maintaining and transmitting a common culture of increasing complexity. Two other social processes intersect with this rising investment, however. First, the influence over learning of the mass and electronic media has become not only competitive but in some respects dominant. Second, as educational institutions themselves develop, competing knowledge enterprises form within them, and the older, larger culture no long remains adequate to contain and coordinate them. Scientists and engineers pull away from the general educational framework, for instance, as the latter fails to change quickly enough to sustain the growth of specialized knowledge bases in each science. Within clusters of the humanities, old agreements about what is worth learning and about the canons of literature and history disintegrate, to be supplanted by competing bodies of knowledge and competing pedagogies. A large university today is no longer what we would call a setting for liberal arts or general education; rather, it is a kind of multiversity and a cafeteria for the dispensing of competing disciplines and professions.

Emile Durkheim (1956) and Willard Waller (1932) had emphasized the centrality of *authority* of the teacher as the key to the school-based transmission of culture. As the mass media accumulated influence during the 1960s, and as youths, four times as numerous as before World War II, began to accumulate social power, schools and universities became increasingly unable to agree on what to teach. Under these circumstances, the authority that had inhered in teachers for centuries before the late 1960s began to crumble. Some of that authority had simply been culturally posited, as the position of teacher carried special properties of respect and deference. Reinforcement derived from the fact that teachers had the authority to reward and punish students, both academically and socially. Their authority came apart under the pressure of student unrest. What was left of it eroded further as students with tastes shaped by thousands of hours of exposure to television and other media tuned out unless teachers were able to incorporate effective routines of entertainment into their classroom instruction. Both technological and cultural change have thus transformed the context of teaching and learning within schools. As schooling has increased sharply in importance in affecting the positioning of students, it has also diminished radically in its capacity to socialize children and youth. Television, along with the mass marketing of products and entertainments for children and youth, overshadow socialization in school and often make the school setting tedious and boring by comparison.

Sociological practitioners began their work on education a century ago, in the tradition of Lester Ward and John Dewey. Their primary initial concern was with the equalization of access to schooling, because of their conviction that making opportunities to learn more free, universal, and inclusive would integrate the social order and profoundly democratize it. Part of this effort, expressed in the monograph, *Who Shall Be Educated?* (Warner and Havighurst 1945), has borne great fruit over the decades.

Yet, across the course of the same century, the very frameworks of schools and colleges have changed. Greater proportions of each generation are enrolled for longer spans of time, and the kinds of diverse programs at all grade levels have multiplied, but the return on the overall investment has been shrinking. So, too, the ability of schools to integrate the society itself has declined, as disputes over which parts of the culture should be transmitted have grown, and disciplines and professions and, indeed, teachers working at different grade levels from early childhood to graduate universities have come to ignore one another and to specialize within ever-narrower divisions of knowledge.

Whether schools and colleges as physical places where students gather to be taught can surmount the contending sources of competition and confusion is raised to a new level of doubt by the advent of distance learning. No educational technology has ever gathered as much volume and momentum as swiftly as has the provision of learning programs over the Internet. Virtual schools and universities are materializing each year through this vehicle; today, thousands of course, certificate, and degree programs are offered for sale, from the level of basic literacy learning through the high school diploma and upward through doctorates. Not all of them are private and commercial, either. California is creating what its government calls the state's own Virtual University of California, and New York offers distance-learning degree programs approved by its Board of Regents.

One sociologist who pioneered in developing computer-based learning was Omar Khayam Moore. As a young junior assistant professor of sociology at Yale University in the 1950s, Moore began to develop what he came to call an "Autotelic Environment," with the technology of his "talking typewriter" built into a converted house trailer (1980). He thought that the fastest and best learning in children occurred under conditions where it was self-motivated and unimpeded by interruptions and interventions from adult humans. His child volunteers would enter the trailer and explore the machines, especially the talking typewriter which responded by neutral computer voice and by recording on a print screen when a child pressed a key. Within days of child-to-machine interaction, children—even three- and four-year-olds, eventually—would learn to form words, to spell, and, on a related electric keyboard, to take simple dictation of sentences. Moore filmed the Autotelic Environment learning experiments with care and began showing the films to groups of professionals around the United States in the late 1950s.

The observable effects were no less than astounding, but when peers began to ask him for experimental evidence, Moore replied that his control groups consisted of all the three- and four-year-olds in the world who could not write, spell, or take verbal dictation. Within a few years, he was denied promotion and tenure at Yale—perhaps because he flouted conventions of research design and was arrogant about it, or perhaps because his work was far too applied to fit the conventions of sociology at that university. Moore took his technology and his trailer to the Edison Company in Pittsburgh, Pennsylvania, where the Talking Typewriter was manufactured and marketed during the 1960s and 1970s. By the 1980s, PCs had become available in schools and homes, and thousands of instructional programs were sold for use by children. To this day, no one in academia or in industry has surpassed Moore's initial accomplishment in demonstrating the enormous potential of self-motivated learning combined with computer assistance.

Sociologists participated in other, related applications of the new technologies in the same era as Moore. In 1959, I was working in the Bureau of Child Research of the University of Kansas. Several of my colleagues, speech psychologists, were pioneering in the design and testing of laboratory environments, including reward machines, in which retarded and autistic boys might learn to speak. Funded heavily by the National Institute of Mental Health, the main project, based at the Parsons, Kansas, State Training School for Boys, utilized verbal learning theory taken from psychologist B. F. Skinner's work to reinforce and shape sounds uttered by the boys.

I visited the laboratory with my colleagues and came away deeply and positively impressed by their progress. Eight- to ten-year-old boys who had never communicated verbally before, or who had spoken with very poor intelligibility, were audibly and visibly succeeding in learning to speak! Small machines stimulated them with recorded sounds; other machines manipulated images, light, and color; and, central to the experiments, a machine rewarded each boy with candy or other food each time he uttered and began to shape sounds into words and sentences.

These experiments were succeeding when all other approaches tried in that era had failed. As my colleagues represented it to me, however, there was a major drawback: the boys learned to speak when in the laboratory, but reverted to silence or mere noise after leaving the program and returning to their regular life routines in the cottages where they resided in groups of thirty or so under the care of adult attendants. The director of the Bureau, Richard Schiefelbusch, asked me to do a field study of the lives of boys outside the laboratory, to see if the sources of unlearning could be identified.

Field research with psychologist Bernard Mackler (Dentler and Mackler 1961) found that cottage attendants and other adult staff in the training school were the sources of the extinction of verbal learning in the boys. They observably punished acts of communication and the assertion of social leadership among the group of boys in a new cottage, thus ensuring that the newcomers would become cautious, passive residents in a setting where they would be institutionalized for the next ten to twelve years. Attendants, drawn from the working population of farmhands on the farms surrounding the school, generally regarded the boys as defective and believed they would prove much more controllable over the years if they learned to be quiet and to obey adult orders. In effect, the staff of the institution had an implicit if unwitting stake in maintaining the students' retardation and disabilities. Sociometric evidence triangulated with cottage observation and records provided strong evidence for this conclusion.

SOME INTERPRETIVE NOTES

This chapter should make plain to all readers that sociologists have participated heavily in education as an institution and a process for more than a century. In the period from 1965 to 1980, this participation reached its peak, as the field of the sociology of education matured into one of the four largest specialties within the membership of the American Sociological Association. If a graduate student enters either a department of sociology degree program or a school of education degree program today, however, the depth and scope of that involvement will usually be lost. How did this come to be, and what can we learn about the process for the future of sociological practice?

A simultaneous decline struck both departments of sociology and schools of education in the period from 1978 to 1990. Employment opportunities in both fields were drying up in most states. Schools of education not only lost enrollment, but also suffered increasing political attacks on their programs.

Vocationalism was overtaking the social sciences in the same period; students who might formerly have majored in sociology were voting with their tuition dollars to major in criminal justice, gerontology and geriatric services, alcohol and drug abuse services, and the like.

Sociology faculty were among the first victims of the retrenchment and revision of faculty and programs in the nation's 1,300 schools and departments of education in the 1980s. Psychology had always dominated those schools anyway, and in the 1980s it rose in relative popularity through counseling degree programs, special education studies, and tests-and-measurements courses.

The sociology of education, moreover, did not figure in the plans of those who worked toward helping departments of sociology survive. The key programs in this difficult period became medical sociology, criminology, and applied sociology. The sociology of education was, with few exceptions among graduate centers, relegated to (at most) two undergraduate course offerings and one or two graduate courses. Sociologists specializing in this subfield dropped substantially in numbers and included diminishing proportions of those under forty years of age who were entering college and university faculties.

Prospective clients for sociological practice in education were disappearing by the thousands during the 1980s as well. Federal investments in public education came under intense criticism during the Reagan administration years, as did previous federal activities in sociologically oriented program planning, evaluation, and improvement projects. Even as the focus for educational policy and services shifted to the states, though, the number of sociologists who were hired or commissioned to work on state and local education issues under state auspices (always a small group) plummeted. International projects grew in this period; otherwise, school district research and planning departments shrank drastically as political leaders took over the enterprise they came to call school reform.

By 1995, however, the gloom was lifting from both fields of activity. Economic prosperity and a mini-boom in annual births combined to renew interest in sociology among college students. Graduate programs in the field expanded again, slowly at first and then swiftly toward the close of the decade. Schools of education continued to be in political disfavor, and a handful of them were disestablished each year during the 1990s, while other sister schools saw yet more reductions in faculty.

In spite of a resurgence of interest in careers in education and in sociology, growth in public education has taken a radically different turn in very recent years. Political leaders in more than half of the states have introduced essentially conservative, mandatory "reforms." An increase in required courses, testing standards for school promotion and graduation, stringent teacher tests, and similar top-down efforts to solve education problem have generated yet another rise in right-wing criticism of public school systems, and fostered support among conservatives for charter schools—schools that function outside the framework of state and local boards and administrative rules—and vouchers for parental use in seeking private or parochial alternatives to local public schools. These are not the sorts of reforms that entail advance research and planning or even process evaluation; they are mere mandates that pass for improvements among parts of the electorate.

In the years just ahead, sociological practice in education will live on and indeed flourish, I believe, but under different labels and through different channels of sponsorship. The need for the utilization of sociological theories, research, and operational methods will grow, not diminish, under conditions of increasingly rapid globalization and high technology growth. Demographic analyses; organizational studies and planning; and evaluations of deep and broad changes in pedagogies generally, and in distance-learning approaches in particular, will all militate for the use of sociological resources.

Practitioners seeking career opportunities in the application of sociology to education will probably not be called sociologists, save for those based in university and college departments of sociology, where incentives for this specialization will be slight. Instead, practitioners who gain elementary or secondary teaching experience, who take challenging course work in administration and educational planning, and who learn the methods of highly applied evaluation research, will be hired in substantial numbers as educational analysts. Those with advanced skills drawn from the high technology of distance learning will most likely lead the pack.

REFERENCES

Aries, P. 1962. *Centuries of Childhood.* New York: Knopf.

Belluck, P. 1999. Reason is sought for lag by blacks in school effort. *New York Times,* 4 July, 1, 12.

Brim, O. G. 1958. *Sociology and the Field of Education.* New York: Russell Sage Foundation.

Cardinale, J. 1990. Teaching dispute resolution to schoolchildren: the persepectives of the educators. M.A. thesis, Department of Sociology, University of Massachusetts at Boston.

Coleman, J. S. 1961. *The Adolescent Society*. New York: Free Press.

Coleman, J. S., et al. 1966. *Equality of Educational Opportunity*. Washington, D.C.: Government Printing Office.

Davis, A. 1947. *Father of the Man*. Boston: Houghton.

Dentler, R. A., D. C. Baltzell, and D. J. Sullivan. 1983. *University on Trial: The Case of the University of North Carolina*. Cambridge, Mass.: Abt Books.

Dentler, R. A., and B. Mackler. 1961. The socialization of institutional retarded children. *Journal of Health and Human Behavior* 2, no. 4: 243–52.

Dentler, R. A., and M. B. Scott. 1981. *Schools on Trial: An Inside Account of the Boston Desegregation Case*. Cambridge, Mass.: Abt Books.

Dodson, D. W. 1952. Educational sociology through twenty-five years. *Journal of Educational Sociology* 26, no. 1: 2–6.

DuBois, W. E. B. 1968. *The Autobiography of W. E. B. DuBois*. New York: International Publishers.

Durkheim, Emile. 1956. *Education and Sociology*. Glencoe, Ill.: Free Press.

Fischer, J. R., et al. 1964. *Desegregating the New York City Public Schools*. New York: Institute of Urban Studies, Teachers College, Columbia University.

Foley, D. 1990. Danger: School zone. *Teacher* 1, no. 8: 57–63.

Frazier, E. F. 1951. *The Negro Family in the United States*. New York: Dryden.

Hallinan, Maureen T., and S. S. Smith, 1989. Classroom characteristics and student friendship cliques. *Social Forces* 67, no. 4: 898–919.

Hallinan, Maureen T., and R. A. Teixeira. 1987. Students' interracial friendships: Individual characteristics, structural effects, and racial differences. *American Journal of Education* 95: 563–83.

Hallinan, Maureen T., and R. A. Williams. 1990. Students' characteristics and the peer-influence process. *Sociology of Education* 63, no. 2: 122–32.

Ianni, F. A. J. 1989. *The Search for Structure*. New York: Macmillan.

Kamarck, E. A., and W. A. Galston. 1990. *Putting Children First: A Progressive Family Policy for the 1990s*. Washington, D.C.: Progressive Policy Institute.

Levine, D. U., and R. J. Havighurst. 1992. *Society and Education*. 8th ed. Boston: Allyn & Bacon.

Miller, W. B. 1973. *Violence by Youth Gangs as a Crime Problem in Major American Cities*. Washington, D.C.: Government Printing Office.

Moore, O. K. February 1980. About talking typewriters, folk models, and discontinuities: A progress report on twenty years of research, development, and application. *Educational Technology* 20, no. 2: 15–27.

Mosteller, F., and D. P. Moynihan, eds. 1972. *On Equality of Educational Opportunity*. New York: Random House.

Orland, M. E. 1990. Demographics of disadvantage: Intensity of childhood poverty and its relationship to educational achievement. In *Access to Knowledge,* edited by J. I. Goodlad and P. Keating. New York: College Entrance Examination Board.

Persell, C. H. 1977. *Education and Inequality.* New York: Free Press.

Robbins, R. 1997. *Sidelines Activist: Charles S. Johnson and the Struggle for Civil Rights.* Jackson, Miss.: University of Mississippi Press.

Rogers, D. 1969. *110 Livingston Street.* New York: Random House.

Slavin, R. E. 1991. Synthesis of research on cooperative learning. *Educational Leadership* 48, no. 5: 72–82.

Taylor, D. G. 1978. Attitudes toward racial integration. *Scientific American* 238, no. 6: 42–49.

Taylor, D. G., and M. J. Alves. 1999. Controlled Choice: Rockford, Illinois, desegregation. *Equity and Excellence in Education* 32, no. 1: 18–30.

Waller, W. 1932. *The Sociology of Teaching.* New York: Wiley.

Warner, W. L., and R. J. Havighurst. 1945. *Who Shall Be Educated?* New York: Harper.

Willie, C. V., M. Alves, and G. Hagerty. September 1996. Multiracial, attractive city schools: Controlled Choice in Boston. *Equity and Excellence in Education* 29, no. 2: 5–19.

Wilson, A. B. 1967. Educational consequences of segregation in a California community. In *Racial Isolation in the Public Schools,* vol. 2, appendix C3. Washington, D.C.: U.S. Commission on Civil Rights/Government Printing Office.

6

Evaluation

INTRODUCTION

As sociologists Peter Rossi, Howard Freeman, and Mark Lipsey define it in their widely used textbook, "Program evaluation is the use of social research procedures to systematically investigate the effectiveness of social intervention programs" (1999, 4). In this chapter I both expand and refine this definition, but it suffices for an introduction to this field of sociological practice. "Social research procedures" is a phrase intended to distinguish between social scientific research methods and techniques and the methods employed in other fields of inquiry. For example, in evaluating musical and theatrical productions, aesthetic, musicological, and dramaturgical methods are appropriate, and they use different standards of evidence and analysis than would social scientific methods. The phrase "social intervention programs" differentiates evaluation from the field of policy and limits it to the assessment of organized efforts to distribute a benefit, prevent a harm, or remedy an inequity. Many social policies are carried out through programs, of course.

Sociologists are currently engaged in evaluating programs in more than a hundred countries around the world. Most of the programs they evaluate are creations of governmental agencies. They include, to give just a few examples, social insurance, welfare services, health care, educational services, housing assistance, and crime prevention and control efforts. Some programs, of course, are those of independent social agencies, foundations, corporations, and grassroots or citizen organizations. Nearly all of them work from the premise that some social needs and social problems can be remedied or mitigated by the implementation of planned interventions. The reasons why sociological practitioners are often drawn into evaluation work, and the kinds of work they do, are explored in this chapter.

HISTORY

Evaluations are as old as recorded history. They first appear as part of the record of physical engineering. Will a pyramid of a certain type prove to be constructable? How goes the effort to build it? If we use this type of navigational technology, will our travel take us to our destination? Applications of astronomy, physics, and mathematics, in other words, opened up the world's earliest pathways toward evaluation. Even the vocabulary—the words and metaphors—we use are byproducts of these fields of engineering: *assess, measure, gauge.* Economic modes of evaluation came next when, in the emerging history of world trade and mercantilism, the fields of accounting, auditing, and actuarial analysis began to evolve some 300 years ago. As industrialization evolved, health care officials began to develop programs of public health evaluations as part of inspectional and investigative campaigns intended to reduce or control the spread of contagious diseases. In some respects, sanitation and vaccination programs were the forerunners of the modern science of program evaluation.

Among the many correlates of industrialization are the rise of the nation-state and the accelerating evolution of modern warfare (Dentler 1971). Twice as many men were killed in battle during World War I as were killed all of the world's major wars between 1790 and 1913, and World War II became a killing ground four times the magnitude of World War I. As whole industrial societies were drawn repeatedly into war in this century, technologies for evaluating weapons, weapons systems, battle strategies and tactics, and personnel selection, training, and performance evolved alongside the other instruments of warfare. The original Binet IQ test was developed in part to select recruits for the French Army in 1913, and a version of it was subsequently used in the United States to weed out conscripts who were below average in intelligence. This assessment tool and the utilization of medical examination data for this purpose produced some politically devastating results in this nation, as it became apparent that levels of educational, mental, and physical fitness were far below what had been assumed before military mobilization began. These and many more specialized tools for personnel assessment were developed and applied during World War II, as the Navy and then the newly created Air Force relied heavily on evaluation as part of their buildup of capabilities.

Evaluation procedures of a crude sort had been devised and used during the Great Depression, to monitor the scope and operation of welfare assistance, Civilian Conservation Corps projects, and the Works Progress Administration. This was, however, a comparatively slight prologue to the expansion of evaluation applications that occurred during World War II. Thus, the field of program evaluation came into its own in the national governments of the West during the 1950s. State and local government agencies lagged far behind federal agencies in this regard, and in the private sector use of the technologies of evaluation continued to be confined to physical engineering and medical programs.

Indeed, it was World War II and its aftermath of public investments in reconstruction—United Nations, the Marshall Plan, the American rebuilding of Japan, and the G.I. Bill, to name just a very few—that pushed program evaluation enterprises toward maturity. The rising fashion in government was to prepare for assessments of what policies and programs worked, and how well and at what cost, as part of making public investments. The formative years for the growth industry of evaluation in the United States and in other Western countries were those from 1950 to 1970.

Governments drew initially upon university faculties for evaluation research. Just as scientific, engineering, and medical faculties had become closely enmeshed with government funding during the course of the war, so this pattern expanded to include the whole range of social and behavioral sciences. The managerial machinery for awarding grants and contracts came into being in the federal agencies for education, welfare, housing and urban development, and labor training by the mid-1950s, and these agencies used procedures copied from the Department of Defense. Professors and teams of graduate students and technical assistants competed for federal funds to carry out evaluations, so frequently that the demand for such services strained the organizational and subcultural capabilities of universities.

The demand for evaluation professionals exploded with the advent of the "Great Society" programs of the Lyndon Johnson era, beginning in 1964. These included the War on Poverty, welfare reforms of enormous scale, Medicare and later Medicaid, expansion of Social Security, educational investments of great magnitude, and so forth. For the first time in the nation's history, nearly every type of federal investment carried with it a mandate for formal evaluation. Much of this work called for independence from the Civil Service, so university-based social scientists were called upon to undertake these new tasks.

Higher education was coping with its own growing pains, however. The children of the Baby Boom triggered by the end of World War II were on their way to college and campus leaders were scrambling desperately to keep up with rising demands for enrollment. The organizational machinery of campuses was straining just to meet these demands, let alone the requests pouring in from federal agencies for research and development services. In addition, the reward structures of universities did not accommodate the patterns of contract evaluation research very well: these included quick start-ups, agreement about strict timetables for delivery of work products, a readiness to accept external supervision, and above all a departure from the highest standard of scholarship, in which scholars pose questions on the basis of their specialized grasp of what would lead to strategic research findings for progress in the discipline. In the colleges of arts and sciences especially, this identification of professorship with basic rather than applied research was very strong, and this standard, rather than public service or teaching, took high priority in the reputational ranking, promotion, and tenure decisions of colleges and universities. Furthermore, evaluation projects are quite simply a hassle. They cannot be fitted easily into teaching schedules and the associated rituals of seminars, graduate examinations, and the like. They often become embroiled in controversies that erupt in the public domain because they are associated closely with pressing issues within the political environment.

In spite of these latent contradictions between university tradition and program evaluation, many universities to this day maintain centers and institutes that carry out evaluative studies. These are especially prevalent at state universities because those organizations have service obligations to the states that fund them. They often include institutes of governmental studies, bureaus of labor economics and of child research, experimental agriculture stations, and public health centers of many kinds, to give just a few examples. From 1965 on, however, more and more firms—both for-profit and non-profit—were established outside of universities in order to work on evaluation contracts awarded by federal, and sometimes by state, agencies.

THE BELTWAY BANDITS

More than 100 contract research and development firms were formed in the United States between 1965 and 1975. Many of these grew up and out of universities yet remained closely tied to them, drawing upon faculty as consulting specialists and upon students from each of the social sciences as recruits. For example, the Stanford Research Institute, known today as SRI International, in Menlo Park, California, began basically as a spinoff from Stanford University. It currently includes more than half a dozen divisions and subsidiaries, ranging from engineering and computer science teams to business management consulting to evaluation services in education and related human service fields. In the latter area, SRI's Center for Education and Human Services specializes in studies of early childhood education, reform issues in elementary and secondary education, innovations in mathematics and science education, higher education, and programs that enhance the ability of communities to meet the needs of children and families.

The Rand Corporation, based in Santa Monica, California, carries out a similar array of research and development projects. It originated as a strategic planning and evaluation service unit for the U.S. Air Force, and many of its operations are classified top secret to this day. Its extension into domestic social program planning and evaluation began in the 1960s and now constitutes a large-scale enterprise.

Abt Associates Incorporated is an East Coast counterpart to SRI and Rand. It began in 1965 by doing contract work in both program evaluation and curriculum development for the U.S. Office of Education; in its first years the staff consisted of about eight social scientists and engineers who worked in offices above a garage in Cambridge, Massachusetts. Clark Abt, the founder, held an undergraduate degree in engineering and a Ph.D. in political science, both from M.I.T., and his company remains symbiotic with that university and with neighboring Harvard University to this day. At its earliest peak of corporate development in 1980, Abt Associates maintained five offices in the United States, Canada, and Europe, and employed more than 1,000 people. At that time, more than 90 percent of its revenues came from federal contracts, most of which were devoted to program evaluation in education, family services, criminal justice, labor training, and health care systems.

In addition to the big firms of this type, the emerging industry of evaluation boasted more than eighty firms that generally employed fewer than twenty people. These often undertook temporary staff expansions in order to carry out national and sometimes international projects. The industry thus began to build a cadre of relatively permanent (and eventually aging) professionals and support personnel, sometimes supplemented by thousands of temporary and shorter-term contract employees, some of whom came to be called *project hoppers*. Overall, it was a very young industry, comparable in many ways to the start-up firms in Silicon Valley of the 1990s. The average age of professional and support staff combined at Abt Associates in 1980 was 28 years, for instance, and many of the firms, including Abt, did not develop pension funds until later in the 1980s.

In the same formative period of the late 1960s, many federal agencies created their own extragovernmental research and development (R&D) institutes and centers. Some of these were mandated by specific legislation. The 1964 Elementary and Secondary Education Act called for the creation of a dozen regional educational laboratories and about ten educational R&D centers to work on school improvement, with a special focus on upgrading the quality of learning opportunities for impoverished and ethnic minority children and youth. The latter units all had intimate ties to colleges and universities. Sister centers were fostered by other federal agencies as part of the War on Poverty and other social policy initiatives.

Both types of firms were distributed across the United States, but the largest number came to be concentrated in Virginia and Maryland, along the beltway around the District of Columbia. Examples include Westat, Mathematica, and the Cosmos Corporation. This put the staffs in readiest reach of their funding sources and facilitated their frequency and quality of interaction with agency staffs. By the late 1970s, these firms had increased so much in density and public policy influence that they were dubbed "Beltway Bandits" by journalists. The label stuck and is still used in the media. Obviously, it connotes a readiness to "hijack" federal governmental functions as well as resources.

Although the projects these firms carried out were for the most part grounded in the social and behavioral sciences, the structure and procedures that evolved to fund and supervise them were close imitations of the forms developed during World War II by the Department of Defense for weapons research and procurement, tactical and strategic planning, and personnel management. This became important because it helped to shape the activity system of social scientific practices in evaluation. It favored quantitative and positivistic approaches and survey technologies, among other influences.

The same period fostered alternative practices as well. Politically progressive and culturally divergent trends were coursing through sociological and psychological networks on the nation's campuses. Grassroots movements of several kinds were at the zenith of their activism, and within this context program evaluators applied anti-positivistic approaches and symbolic interactionist concepts in the assistance they gave members of such movements. Alternative schools, storefront academies, holistic and homeopathic health care, communes, and other expressions of counterculturalism joined in a growing skepticism about Big Government. From the countercultural viewpoint, the evaluation industry was seen as a patsy to the Establishment, even as sociological practitioners were becoming advocate-technicians for alternative forms of social action. Community action, decentralization of social controls of all kinds, and a quest for ways to restore the cohesiveness of primary organization all adopted program evaluation techniques in the service of their quests.

Some of the progressivism of the first decade in the evaluation industry affected the lives and work of professionals within the big firms. For example, late in the 1960s, the staff at Abt Associates voted to shun military and defense industry-related contracts, as an expression of anti-war fervor. Abt Associates and other firms were placed on a Defense Department blacklist for this reason, and could not have received funding from this, the largest segment of the federal government, if they had tried. There were other facets to the progressivism of the era: evaluators began to avoid disciplinary labels and to collaborate across the conventional boundaries of their specialties, for one. Teams made up of staff from several fields worked with norms that valued the ideal of the skilled generalist—an ideal that had been in sustained retreat within each of the social sciences since the 1920s. Evaluation teams also tried to write their reports in user-friendly ways that differed markedly from the expository conventions of professional journals and papers presented at annual meetings.

The same period spawned the formation of evaluation centers in most of the world's nation-states. These came increasingly to be required as part of loans and investments made by the World Bank and the International Monetary Fund. Bankers and economists within these and sister agencies insisted that a wide range of investments in infrastructure, agriculture, education, and health care be evaluated as to effectiveness as well as monitored for accountability. Cross-national and international studies were greatly stimulated in this process, and thousands of American social scientists began to break out of the cocoons of monolingual and North American-based knowledge that had contained them for several generations.

Evaluation research is an activity that can cut both ways politically. In periods of expanding public enthusiasm for governmental interventions and funded services, as in the 1962–1970 period, evaluations are undertaken as part of a search for better ways to design and conduct those programs and as part of a demonstration of their worth. As the political pendulum swings (as it began to do leftward in 1960, and then hard to the right in England and the United States in the years from 1981 to 1992), evaluations are mounted as part of an effort to reconsider public investments and to critique them harshly enough to justify policy revision and program termination. In periods of centrist policies and politics, evaluation may be used to advocate for maintenance of the status quo and for fine-tuning of public programs.

ERA OF THE RIGHT-WING SWING

Sociologists were taken somewhat by surprise by the scope and intensity of the swing toward political and cultural conservatism, both symbolized and ushered in by the Margaret Thatcher and Ronald Reagan regimes in England and the United States. The discipline is less than impressive in its ability to forecast megatrends, although it includes a subsection of individuals who call themselves futurists and who study such trends. Perhaps the tradition of specialization and focus on service to the discipline itself, and service to the academy around it, distracts most sociologists' attention from the political environment. In any event, sociologists found themselves constrained by static or downsizing conditions within their colleges and universities during the 1980s. Enrollments shrank; campuses that had overbuilt in earlier years could not be maintained effectively; and faculty positions were cut back rather than expanded year by year. Thus the era of postwar expansion came to an end for higher education and for academic sociology. The shifting political environment also cut deeply into the evaluation industry. Abt Associates shrank from 1,000 to 500 employees and dissolved some of its branch offices between 1981 and 1983. Of the hundred or so firms engaged in federal contract evaluations, about thirty failed and disappeared. Those that remained began to take on increasing amounts of business work, as well as state and local government projects, in an attempt to close the gap created by much-reduced federal dollar amounts.

With faculty appointments heading toward zero, and with evaluation work within the industry shrinking, the years from 1982 through 1990 were especially difficult for sociology and the other social sciences. The Beltway Bandit firms did not suffer as much because the federal civil service underwent both downsizing and morale degradation in this period; the independent firms took on increasing amounts of outsourced work because there was no one available within agencies to do it. Much of this work was in the administrative support tradition, however, and did not directly involve the application of the social sciences. Nationwide and even internationally during this period, however, graduate enrollments in sociology shrank and large-scale evaluation studies became increasingly rare. What work on evaluation projects remained available was still reduced, and funding was severely restricted.

IMPACT OF CUTBACKS IN SOCIOLOGY

Federal investments in program evaluation had led, between 1955 and 1980, to a strong emphasis in research design on the value of experiments. These designs presupposed a social program in which benefits were not universal, but rather targeted at selectively eligible subpopulations; thus, the evaluator could assign recipients randomly to experimental and control groups at the outset of a new program, essentially in the applied scientific and statistical traditions established earlier in the century in agriculture and medicine. The obviously superior features of this design were (1) that the evaluator could gauge, reasonably authoritatively, whether a gain in the control subjects was in fact the result of programmatic rather than other interventions or environmental forces; and (2) that the evaluator could get insight into some of the main causes of the gain.

A famous example of this approach comes from the New Jersey-Pennsylvania Income-Maintenance Experiment (Kershaw and Fair 1976). As part of the War on Poverty, this program provided cash income payments to poor families in order to test whether this reduced incentives to work. Some eight experimental conditions consisted of different income guarantees and the rates at which the payments were taxed—that is, adjusted to earnings achieved by each family. The experiment was conducted with 1,300 families who were found to be eligible within 4 communities in the 2 states, with households being assigned randomly to one of the 8 experimental groups or to a control group that received no cash payments. The experiment was carried on for three years but was then cut off by the government. Among various findings of importance for social policy, the experiment showed that the work effort of the experimental group families decreased by 5 percent.

The large-scale experimental evaluation tradition persists. A team of Abt Associates evaluators (St. Pierre et al. 1999) reported on their evaluation of a federal program funded by the Administration on Children, Youth and Families within the U.S. Department of Health and Human Services. The program goal was to deliver a comprehensive range of social services to at-risk families from within the framework of case management. The evaluation was explicitly mandated by Congress as part of the funding legislation and was awarded under contract after a formal competition in which a host of firms participated.

The research questions concerned the effectiveness of the case-managed services in meeting the developmental needs of children, economic self-sufficiency of mothers, mothers' parenting skills, and variation in effects across program sites and population subgroups. The evaluation design assigned 2,213 families to the experimental program groups and 2,197 to control groups whose members received other locally delivered services but not the federal program package. The families were followed and data collected for a five-year period beginning in 1990. Measurements were frequent during those years. Meticulous comparative analyses of the evidence forced the conclusion that the program *did not produce any important positive effects on participating families.* For an intervention that cost, on average, $15,678 per family per year, this finding had enormous policy significance.

Two other evaluation research designs have long been more frequently used. The first is the quasi-experimental design, in which the experimental group participating in the program is compared with one or more control or comparison groups that are not. Random assignment to one group or the other does not figure in the design; rather, the control group is selected because it has some known and relevant similarities to the experimental group. The members of the two or more groups are matched on social characteristics or, more commonly today, equated through a process of statistical adjustments.

The quasi-experimental design gives the evaluator much more freedom to collect and analyze evidence than does the experimental design, and ethical as well as political difficulties entailed in assigning members to groups, and thus denying some eligible beneficiaries the products or services of the program, are avoided. It lacks the power of analytic validation common to experimental designs, however, because the evaluator cannot be fully confident that the effects the study locates are the result of the program.

A second alternative to the experiment is time series analysis. In this method, data are gathered along a time line that stretches from a period before the program began, through the period during its delivery, and beyond. Analysis is then concentrated on whether a substantial—that is, significant—change in the indicator(s) is shown somewhere along the line. When feasible, more than one indicator is utilized, and graphs permitting comparison with other settings in which no program or some other programs took place may augment the analysis. The most obvious limitation of this design is that the evaluator cannot be confident that the changes shown in the indicator are the result of the program intervention.

Both of the experimental evaluations described earlier in this section were conducted by evaluation firms contracted to work independently of the funding agencies and the program service delivery firms and institutions. The conceptual model underlying this arrangement requires organizational and advocacy distance to be maintained between sponsors, operators, and evaluators, in the interest of objectivity. The model presumes that agency clients have formulated, on paper or in their minds, what the intention of intervention in a problematic situation is, how they plan to intervene, and what results they anticipate. The evaluator then comes into the setting and fits a research design to the goals, aims, and procedures planned by the clients.

Features of all the designs are often as exasperating to fulfill as the requirements for experimental design themselves. So ill-prepared for evaluation are most clients that the Urban Institute began to introduce alternative approaches through a process called *evaluability assessment* (Wholey 1979). This process begins with a period of co-planning in which the features of a program are described and rendered in words and diagrams; the program is assessed for the feasibility of its being evaluated; and the eventual uses, by stakeholders and related clients, of evaluation findings of various kinds are formulated in advance.

As formal and systematic as this sounds, the evaluability assessment in fact brings the evaluator into the circle of program planning and preliminary analysis. It often leads to modification in the program and involves the evaluator in the task of building consensus among stakeholders as to what the program aims to accomplish and how it will intervene. Most parts of the process are qualitative and cannot offer the experimental, quantitative features so prized by the traditional evaluator. Also, evaluability assessments often draw the evaluator into revising the approaches and attitudes of clients so that evaluation is approved and facilitated.

Cutbacks in public investments in social programs; reversals of change-inducing program efforts by political progressives; hostility toward federal governmental initiatives in social programs; and a negative change in client views toward social science all contributed to stimulating fundamental shifts in evaluation practice after the early 1980s. There was nothing linear about this trend, however. Over the same years, computer software development was accelerating tremendously. This evolution, combined with the advent of the desktop personal computer, made statistical analysis affordable and feasible as it had never been in previous decades.

By the 1990s, moreover, the mass introduction of the Internet made access to huge electronic databases equally convenient. Census data, as well as both national and cross-national survey data, became easily obtainable. One of the results was a sharp decline in field work and firsthand data gathering and a consequent increase in secondary analysis of these increasingly accessible electronic data sets.

SOCIOLOGISTS AS PROGRAM EVALUATORS

I have noted that program evaluations are done by a very diverse variety of professionals. What, if any, distinctive contribution do sociologists make to work in this field? Part of the answer to this question is shaped by history. Fifty years ago, sociologists were most closely aligned, relative to all the social and behavioral sciences, with the social service and social control fields of social work, community development, and criminology. Thus, as the demand for evaluations arose in these fields, sociologists were the best informed and most available researchers to be called upon by practitioners. It is out of this relationship, for instance, that Ernest Burgess and others in the Chicago School of sociology began to do applied research, in conjunction with Jane Addams and Hull House, on juvenile crimes and eventually on parole prediction methods in the 1920s.

Secondly, sociologists developed social theories of organization, deprivation, and interpersonal relations that are often very well suited to interpreting programs and to accounting for their successes and failures. Third, and perhaps most crucially in the early years of professionalization, American sociologists pioneered in survey, field research, and analytic approaches to evaluative evidence. These distinctive resources have come to be shared widely with other specialists and skilled generalists alike in the years since 1965, and they are now part of graduate curricula in education, public administration, business management, labor relations, and nursing, to name a few of the specialties that have incorporated them.

To give one example, Deborah Henderson and Anne B. Henderschott (1993) conducted a three-year evaluation of a privately funded adolescent parenting and pregnancy prevention program in a large northeastern city. In their first year of study, they worked from what they regarded as a value-free approach, accepting the criteria for service delivery and success from the white, middle-class professionals who managed the program. Their first-year report of preliminary findings generated considerable controversy:

[We reported] that confident assertions about the number of recurring pregnancies could not be made because evidence . . . existed which indicated that some of the participants had terminated a second pregnancy. . . . Teenage mothers who became pregnant again and chose to continue their pregnancy became ineligible for services and were, thus, terminated from the program. But, participants who chose to abort a subsequent pregnancy were allowed to continue. (270)

As a result of this first report, funding for the program entered a period of intense political dispute based on controversies surrounding the abortion issue. Their third-year report was different. It used extensive qualitative data, based on observations and interviews with program participants and staff members, to show sponsors and other stakeholders the several ways in which members of these groups faced the challenges of their lives and defined their situations from the basis of divergent value preferences. They essentially defused the abortion question by, in their words, "taking the role of the other" in depicting the process of adolescent parenting and of program service delivery.

In another example, Theodore A. Lamb and Keric B. O. Chin (1992) reported on an evaluative analysis of an Air Force training program. These sociologists do their training analyses and training evaluation work from within the U.S. Air Force. As they note, most designs for training are grounded in psychological theories, and their report focuses on ways in which sociological concepts improve the ability of evaluative analysts to assess training programs. What they concentrate upon are groups, organizational frameworks through which training is planned and delivered, whole societies, and the sociology of the world system. Their report on assessing a repair and maintenance technician training program used what they called the "analytic onion" of these social concepts, and they worked through layer after layer of this onion in interpreting their findings. Indeed, they were so encouraged by their results that they turned to yet another "layer," which they called "the space system," to help Air Force senior planners deal with a future in which the colonization of space becomes a part of their client's regular mission.

EMPOWERMENT AND INCLUSIVE EVALUATION

Just as a kind of corporate industry in evaluation took shape in the 1960s, so the professionals who took part began to organize themselves in the 1970s. By the close of that decade, they had formed the American Evaluation Association (AEA), which had its own bylaws, membership dues, conventions, and journals. Twenty years later, the AEA boasted more than 2,300 members. Its main journal, once named *Evaluation Practice,* had matured into *The American Journal of Evaluation,* and its members had formulated guidelines for ethical practice.

One group within the AEA began to weave together various threads of social scientific practice, which had existed since the 1930s yet had played a relatively minor role in the wartime and postwar emergence of that practice. These included participatory research in sociology, action research in anthropology, and empowerment theories in education and community development. According to David Fetterman (1999), the shared aim of these traditions is to give a voice to the people the practitioners work with and to convey that voice to policy makers.

In empowerment evaluation, the evaluator becomes a collaborator and facilitator rather than an expert or counselor. The professional evaluator's knowledge and skills are not imposed on the clients or beneficiaries; rather, they become resources that are made available to the participating communities of groups and individuals. A number of evaluators have written articles and books describing this approach to empowerment (Zimmerman et al. 1992; Zimmerman and Rappaport 1988; Dunst, Trivette, and LaPointe 1992). These writers have pointed out that the change in approach involves closing the distance between program agents, participants, and evaluators. The latter invest themselves in program formulation, planning, public relations, training, and other technical assistance. As Fetterman noted, "The entire group—not a single individual, not the external evaluator or an internal manager—is responsible for conducting the evaluation. The group thus can serve as a check on its own members. . . . The evaluator is a co-equal in this endeavor, not a superior and not a servant" (Fetterman 1999, 3–4).

Inclusive evaluation is a similar departure from the evaluation tradition of the 1950s. Donna M. Mertens summarized the inclusive approach concisely, reviewed its current literature, and explored how it creates tensions by its emphasis on including the voices of clients—essentially of marginalized beneficiaries—in the evaluation process (1999). Her article expresses the tension eloquently:

The evaluator should avoid advocacy when it is defined as " . . . taking the views or interests of one group and always championing them over others, regardless of the findings of the evaluation' (House and Howe 1998, 235). However, in order to be inclusive of marginalized groups, evaluators need to struggle with issues of oppression, discrimination, and power differences, and still walk the tightrope of avoiding the bias associated with a position of advocacy. . . . I do not want to see the evaluation community avoid dealing with these important issues by using the labels of advocacy, political motivation, or ideological or ontological nihilism to dismiss efforts to represent validly the viewpoints of those with the least power. (Mertens 1999, 3)

Both empowerment and inclusiveness evaluators believe fervently in the democratic process. They work diligently to square their search for ways to join stakeholders and program participants with the canons of social scientific research: namely, objectivity, intellectual detachment as opposed to advocacy, reliability, and validity. They believe these aims can be reconciled. Fetterman, Mertens, and other evaluators who endorse these approaches believe that evaluators should help to clarify their roles in the program creation and delivery process by showing sponsors and participants alike that they are *not* decision makers or advocates, but rather facilitators and coordinators of the fact-gathering and evidence-interpreting process. They also conceive of empowerment and inclusion taking place within a context in which the agency and its stakeholders want to cooperate, and where readiness to modify the program as it goes along is high.

In my opinion, these approaches are evolving adaptations of evaluation practice. They tend to take place under circumstances where funding is sharply limited, random assignment of subjects in the experimental tradition is programmatically or ethically not feasible, and where much smaller-scale, more qualitative evaluations are desired by sponsors. Here, the evaluators become a kind of multipurpose professional. They provide advice, facilitation, collaborative support, and feedback to agencies about the needs and viewpoints of beneficiaries, and ultimately help plan and refine programs. As a result, the evaluators may be relied upon more fully; their findings may be utilized more earnestly; and their services may be retained for longer periods than when independence and objectivity seem to require distance from stakeholders.

As with other adaptations of professional practices, participatory, empowerment, and inclusion models offer both gains and setbacks to the practice of sociology. The gains are inherent in what we have described. They include more organizational harmony, better representation of participants in the evidence, more opportunities to revise and refine program services and delivery, and the possibility of increased utilization of the services of evaluators and more attention paid to their findings. The setbacks include an unmistakable blurring of the lines between the evaluative function and related program operations, with a decreased emphasis on systematic research as contrasted with program assistance. The occasions when sponsors and stakeholders want collaboration as distinguished from advocacy are comparatively few, especially in times when social programs are under generic stress and political crosspressures. The checks and balances available to teams of evaluators are often scarce at the very time when the teams most need revenues and income for continuing their livelihoods.

The pros and cons of evaluative approaches are also debated constantly within circles of practitioners. Part of the debate concerns the extent to which evaluation may reasonably depart from the tradition of systematic social research and still be considered part of the framework of science. The same debate extends into the heart and core of marketing and consumer research and into survey-based public opinion research. The tools used in these offspring of the social and behavioral sciences—polls, focus groups, interviews, questionnaires, lab observation—can be bent somewhat at will. Questions can be slanted, focus group formation can be twisted, and so on. Just as the research process can be distorted in the service of the customer or client, so may technical assistance, training, advice, and advocacy. Of equal moment in the debates among professionals, careers and egos alike sometimes get attached to a point of view and a strong preference for a particular approach. For example, one that emphasizes the maintenance of distance and independence by the evaluator, versus one that prefers close collaboration and interdependence with the program agents; or between those who dearly love quantitative methods in analysis and those who love qualitative methods—quite apart from the fact that both have merits and may be used in a variety of combinations in program evaluation.

The overall alternative to the competing claims among stakeholders and among practitioners is an academic vacuum. Withdrawal from the welter of claims and rejection of the climate of social and political controversy that often surrounds program evaluation work may offer the peace of the classroom, the library carrel, and the scholar's den, but this peace can prove to be monastic—quiet and conducive to meditation, but also isolative, boring, and possibly unproductive.

EVALUATION BEYOND RESEARCH

Evaluation research has become an established activity worldwide. Governments and their agencies at all levels conduct evaluations or commission them routinely today. Human service institutions—from colleges and universities to community development agencies in the nonprofit sector—often undertake evaluations, and financial investors require them as part of large-scale loans and grants for public projects. After what is now a half-century of maturing experience, the very idea of evaluative activity has gradually become transformed. Research remains central to the enterprise, but a number of other services have been added.

Many evaluators today go beyond the confines of research to engage in program planning and design, actual program service administration, training and technical assistance about operations, and consultative help with employee morale, program reputation, public relations, and advocacy. Part of this adaptive evolution is probably the result of client dissatisfaction with the research function. There is a large literature on the frustrations inherent in communicating and reporting the findings of evaluations (Torres, Preskill, and Piontek 1997). Drawing on the results of a survey of AEA members, Torres and her associates found that half of the evaluations conducted by sample respondents were internally organized and conducted, whereas the textbooks and journal literature give heavy emphasis to external evaluation research. They also found that most evaluators feel very pressed for time—that is, they do not get the resources convertible into work hours to permit full completion of their studies, and they do not get sufficient time and attention from their clients. In fact, a majority of the evaluators, particularly those with less than six years of experience, expressed disappointment that so little feedback is provided by clients and stakeholders to their reports; they report that what clients prefer is a very brief memorandum and some oral or photographic summary of a few key findings rather than a genuine technical report.

At the core of evaluation practice, then, is the continuing realization that the fruits of research labor are seldom consumed and rarely digested and incorporated into policy, program, or operating decisions that involve changes in client or stakeholder behavior. Questions about the *utilization* of evaluation research results abound and indeed haunt the field of practice. Under this circumstance, evaluators have come to search for ways to become more useful to clients under the terms and conditions the clients prefer. It is at this juncture that what we might term the evaluation research ideal gets compromised.

Within colleges and universities, social scientists who have expertise in evaluation research often adapt by turning to other scholarly pursuits. They do policy studies, turn to the kinds of basic research they were trained to do originally, and so on. Within contract research firms, the skilled generalists who make up the core of the professional staff turn gradually toward management consulting, program planning, and quasi-administrative services to clients, while remaining on the alert for opportunities to do evaluations.

The potential for corruption rises when professional evaluators diffuse or multiply their roles. Thirty years ago, an applied sociologist who founded and directed three firms discovered to his extreme dismay what this could mean. He created a program evaluation research firm specializing in education. As the firm grew rapidly, he realized there was a pressing demand among his clients for program planning assistance; therefore, he created a program planning firm. As this second company flourished, his clients joined him in creating a third firm that trained their personnel to carry out the plans. The three firms were interactively circular: the sociologist would bring his very preliminary findings from evaluation to the clients and indicate that continuation of their program would probably result in no benefits to students. He would then invite the client to request an alternative program plan from his second firm. After that plan was purchased, the clients would comment that the plan looked promising—if only they had staff members who were able to carry it out. The sociologist would then offer to contract, through his third firm, to provide this training. Over time, the movement from preliminary evaluation, to planning, to training, become increasingly circular and repetitive. Eventually, he was indicted, tried, convicted, and sentenced to prison in federal court for fraud and exploitation of his clients.

The paradox is that this is essentially a model for much of the work carried out by management consulting firms, public relations corporations, and contract research firms—yet they are not indicted for fraud or exploitation because they offer combinations of this trio of professional services, within a single package or as a contract containing a range of future considerations and options. The analogy here is to the professions of law and medicine, where a bundle of services is developed on the same premises and often by the same learned professionals. It is the same with many engineering firms. But the model of a scientific research laboratory, which seems to undergird many parts of the evaluation research tradition, assumes that the scientist will focus in a highly specialized way upon the inquiries peculiar to her discipline and the laboratory. Even this model is outdated by the nature of the growth of the scientific enterprise today, of course. But as long as evaluation of social programs takes place within a framework of systematic social research, the scientific research laboratory model will be helpful. When the evaluator comes to do planning, training, and management consulting in conjunction with evaluating, the framework loses part of its pertinence and potency.

The emerging alternative is suggested in an article by Mildred A. Morton (1998), whose title is Management Sociologist. She works as a consultant in the Washington, D.C. metropolitan area, where she has specialized in "facilitating the communication of research for various government and private sector organizations" (93). She does not ordinarily carry out the research she facilitates; rather, she interprets and summarizes findings reached by other researchers whose technical reports are too complex and too long to be of use to the various client managers. As Morton put it, she helps to clarify the policy implications of program evaluations; synthesizes the "essence" of complex change efforts; facilitates agency or corporate understanding of research findings, and promotes decisions to take action. She thinks of this as "an expanded role for sociologists in the dissemination and application of research" (96). The special value of her perspective is that it highlights the ways in which sociological practitioners today tend to combine evaluation work with a host of related consultative services.

A more detailed explication of this fusion of roles is given by clinical sociologists George W. Dowdall and Diane M. Pinchoff (1994) in an article on the relation between management and evaluation research within the professional staff of a psychiatric hospital:

Working in a large psychiatric hospital, the sociologist operates in two roles—researcher and manager. As researcher, the sociologist uses the principles and methods of sociology to plan, monitor, and evaluate programs, collecting and analyzing data, formulating and testing hypotheses, and developing recommendations for corrective action. This work is most often done within the context of the hospital's quality assurance or total quality management (TQM) program. . . . As a member of the management team, the sociologist uses the principles and methods of sociology to develop data collection, analysis and reporting systems to meet the clinical, programmatic, fiscal and policy-making needs of administration. (1994, 177)

Their article stresses their conviction that textbooks and other literature about the role of sociologists in evaluation generally share the unifying theme of graduate study in the discipline: commitment to the discipline as a distinctive science, identification with the model of scientific inquiry, and a focus toward drawing upon sociological theories as the guiding source of hypotheses. Dowdall and Pinchoff contrast this with the real world they inhabit as part of senior management at the Buffalo Psychiatric Center, a large psychiatric hospital in New York. In their positions they are not identified as sociologists, and their peers, who share in moving away from service to their disciplines as well, know them as contributors to management operations. Service delivery monitoring and program evaluations are simply part of the hospital's ongoing efforts to make its mission and functioning effective for the mentally ill.

This blurring of boundaries is far from limited to sociology. It takes place today in most professions. Half of those who graduate from university-based theological schools do not enter the ministry, for instance. Half of those who graduate from schools of law do not subsequently practice law as members of law firms or corporate law offices; many do not practice law at all. Two-thirds of those who graduate from schools of public administration and public affairs do not enter federal or state civil service, but work instead for nonprofit service and advocacy agencies. Among social and behavioral scientists, the most fully expanded roles are those occupied by clinical psychologists. This applied section of the discipline is modeled after roles in medicine, and clinical psychologists are trained to diagnose both individual and community pathologies, to treat them therapeutically, to do scientific research, and to teach and supervise students. As specialization within occupational settings has increased in recent decades, many clinical psychologists find they are not situated to carry on or to sustain all these roles, but the model persists nonetheless. Many practitioners in clinical sociology advocate for this model and regard themselves as performers of just such expanded and multiple roles. In this framework, as in the evaluation industry's emphasis upon skilled generalists, evaluation becomes one among many activities carried on concurrently by individual and team professionals alike.

CONCLUSION

Sociological practice in program evaluation is wholly consistent with the founding vision of the discipline: scientific knowledge, theories, and methods should be applied to social phenomena in order to understand, control, and predict their dynamics. When the task is carried out well, the result should be an improvement of some small part of the human condition. More has been accomplished in developing the science of evaluation in the past fifty years than was achieved in the century that went before. This chapter has profiled the swift evolution of this specialty and illustrated its achievements and circumstantial limitations.

I have dealt only a little bit with the implications of the fact that program evaluation is done within a political environment and carries with it a series of enduring ethical dilemmas. The environment is most frequently the one that surrounds federal and state governments, although obviously evaluation inquiry may be carried out by nongovernmental groups and institutions. Both in the United States and abroad, however (if one sets aside private business and industry), perhaps 90 percent of the activity of evaluation research has been sponsored and funded by governmental agencies.

Two major corollaries follow from this fact. First, the practicing evaluator tends most often to be employed in the service of government; hence, the opportunity to exert full intellectual and political independence is substantially reduced. Efforts at empowerment and inclusion evaluation are for the most part efforts to counter this circumstance and to find ways to give voice to the needs and interests of those who are targeted by, and sometimes neglected in the course of, governmentally sponsored programs. Secondly, the evaluator whose work departs too far from convention—in methods, conceptualization of the program itself, and above all, in findings—will seldom be invited to conduct a second or a third study.

The ethical challenges stem in major part from the nature of the political environment. How may the evaluator preserve confidentiality for his participants when his data are owned by a government agency or subject to discovery in the course of litigation? Who decides what is a tolerable burden for an evaluation project to impose upon participants? When is this decision shaped essentially by political considerations? Are the findings from an evaluation to be shared with stakeholders, including beneficiaries and staff service providers, or may they be withheld for a time (or even permanently) by policy makers? These and a host of associated ethical questions surround the contemporary evaluative process.

Some of these questions are addressed by ethical standards and guidelines developed by professional organizations. The American Sociological Association, the American Evaluation Association, the Society for Applied Sociology, and the Sociological Practice Association, among others, have guidelines as well as procedures for examining issues of compliance among members. Federal government agencies also have standards intended to deal with some of these questions. There is always a difference, however, between formal and informal behavior. The formal framework often deals with what should take place and establishes norms and procedures for what should occur, whereas informal practices often depart, sometimes extremely, from those norms. To some extent, the gap between these two levels is greatest when the programs under scrutiny are the most politically and ethically sensitive: crime control and corrections, welfare services, health care services, and programs that seek to reduce ethnic, gender, and class inequities.

Those who become preoccupied with these political and ethical challenges, to the point of nonparticipation in evaluation projects, are mistaking contextual sensitivity for the identification of what is most important. The alternatives to the use of social and behavioral knowledge in assessing programs are unequivocally worse than the most dismal outcomes we can imagine for the tradition of scientific evaluation. Ideological dogmatism, trial and error, peremptory and arbitrary exercises of authoritarian judgment, and libertarian modes of political neglect and avoidance are, for most sociologists, worse sloughs of despair than evaluation will ever become.

REFERENCES

Dentler, R. A. 1971. War and modern society. Chapter 33 in *Society Today,* 495–507. Del Mar, Calif.: CRM Books.

Dowdall, G., and D. M. Pinchoff. 1994. Evaluation research and the psychiatric hospital: Blending management and inquiry in clinical sociology. *Clinical Sociology Review* 12: 175–88.

Dunst, C. J., C. M. Trivette, and N. LaPointe. 1992. Toward clarification of the meaning and key elements of empowerment. *Family Science Review* 5, no. 1: 111–30.

Fetterman, D. 1999. Empowerment evaluation: An introduction. <http://www.stanford.edu/davidt/>.

Henderson, D., and A. B. Henderschott. 1993. Taking the role of the other in designing and disseminating evaluation research: A case study. *Sociological Practice Review* 3, no. 4: 268–71.

House, E. R., and K. R. Howe. 1998. The issue of advocacy in evaluations. *American Journal of Evaluation* 19, no. 2: 233–36.

Kershaw, D., and J. Fair. 1976. *The New Jersey Income-Maintenance Experiment.* Vol. 1. New York: Academic Press.

Lamb, T. A., and K. B. O. Chin. 1992. The analytic onion: Examining Air Force training issues from different levels of analysis. *Sociological Practice Review* 3, no. 3: 119–25.

Mertens, D. M. 1999. Inclusive evaluation: Implications of transformative theory for evaluations. *American Journal of Evaluation* 20, no. 1: 1–14.

Morton, M. A. 1998. From research to policy: Roles for sociologists: Psychological empowerment. *Clinical Sociology Review* 16: 93–96.

Rossi, P. H., H. E. Freeman, and M. W. Lipsey. 1999. *Evaluation: A Systematic Approach.* 6th ed. Thousand Oaks, Calif.. Sage Publications.

St. Pierre, R. G., J. I. Layzer, B. D. Goodson, and L. S. Bernstein. 1999. The effectiveness of comprehensive case management interventions: Evidence from the national evaluation of the Comprehensive Child Development Program. *American Journal of Evaluation* 20, no. 1: 15–34.

Torres, R., H. S. Preskill, and M. E. Piontek. 1997. Communicating and reporting: Practices and concerns of internal and external evaluators. *Evaluation Practice* 18, no. 2: 105–26.

Wholey, J. S. 1979. *Evaluation: Promise and Performance.* Washington, D.C.: Urban Institute.

Zimmerman, M. A., B. A. Israel, A. J. Schulz, and B. Checkoway. 1992. Further explorations in empowerment theory. *American Journal of Community Psychology* 20, no. 6: 707–27.

Zimmerman, M. A., and J. Rappaport. 1988. Citizen participation, perceived control, and psychological empowerment. *American Journal of Community Psychology* 20, no. 6: 725–50.

7

Closing Notes

This book presented just a few of the realms of practice in which contemporary sociologists engage most frequently. Others include psychotherapeutic or sociotherapeutic services, health service systems, community organizing and planning, criminal justice support systems, and applications of demography to questions of policy and equity. Someone studying sociology in most colleges and universities of the world today would hear very little about any of this, for two reasons. First, the cultural norm among academic sociologists, especially in the United States, is strongly toward maintaining the field as a kind of basic science. Second, there is a lag between what takes place in the world and thinking within the academy.

We need to remind ourselves often that there are thousands of sociologically educated women and men who are working in settings where they draw daily upon their sociological knowledge and skills but where this fact is not built into their job titles or the perceptions of colleagues and other staff. The number of these sociologists exceeds by far the number employed today as professors and university research associates. This fact is not evident at a meeting of the old-line disciplinary associations, however. The American Sociological Association and the regional and state associations, such as the Eastern, annually include a few sessions on applied topics, and there are occasional workshops for training in research or organizational consulting skills, but these were uncommon until the 1990s. It is thus not surprising that thousands of those who are not members and who work in nonacademic settings believe that ASA meetings contain nothing of value or pertinence for them. It was during the decade of the 1990s that the Sociological Practice Association and the Society for Applied Sociology became more visible and offered a greater variety of resources and networks through their meetings and newsletters. When combined, however, these evolving associations include fewer than a thousand nonacademics as members, leaving the same thousands in the workplace without sociological affiliations.

The proportion of sociologists who continue to care primarily for their field as academic and nonapplied teachers has declined substantially over the past twenty years. During the same period, university programs have become increasingly vocational and thus practical, particularly as schools of management, allied health care, public affairs, and criminology came to the forefront. Sociologists who remain in or seek positions in universities thus go into these professional schools and leave the colleges of arts and sciences behind. Meanwhile, those colleges have become increasingly vocational.

Many core courses in sociology continue to fail to reflect this change, even as many of these are used as service courses for students enrolled in the professional schools. The interventionist, planning, action, and advocacy features of sociology as a kind of engineering domain remain broadly and generally misunderstood by those who teach the core courses. The transition to a different future is at hand, however.

Within the coming decade, I anticipate the advent of courses within arts-and-science colleges and throughout professional schools in sociotherapy, community change and its induction, attitude change and the induction of structural changes in societies, technical assistance procedures and training approaches for organizations, and a rising range of courses in policy and program evaluation. Sociologists who have maintained affiliations with their applied organizations and who have published in the practice journals will be prepared to lead this change. Those who stay planted in the academic tradition, and those who have marginalized themselves by entering job and career paths in which identification with sociology offers no obvious or short-term gain, will not shape this future, but rather will tend to merge into and become members of other occupations and professions.

Graduate training in applied sociology today stresses a kind of two-tiered approach. For a segment of perhaps a fifth of those enrolled, the degree programs offer preparation in research design, data analysis, and above all, opportunities to perfect skills in the computer-based management and utilization of large-scale data sets. These students obtain posts in federal and state governmental agencies and applied research organizations of many kinds. The jobs are well paid and highly competitive; they demand evidence of growing involvement of the novice in data processing.

A second fifth of enrolled graduates move through the M.A. programs and into jobs in program and human service management and planning. These positions are quite similar to those taken by graduates of social work degree programs. They pay less than the analytic, computer-centered positions, but they are observably more gratifying for graduates who are not keenly motivated to do quantitative research. Other graduates gravitate toward human service positions—whether in counseling, group homes, homeless shelters, parole and probation offices, correctional institutions, or health care providing agencies—where employment demands continue to outstrip the availability of certified personnel from other degree programs.

Joyce Iutcovich (1997) has pointed out the five major challenges facing sociological practitioners in the opening years of the twenty-first century. These are examined here from the point of view of one concerned with how new graduates will enter the field in the decades just ahead. She begins by giving first priority to the proposition that sociology must become a profession. She argues that it is not presently a profession because sociologists lack a monopoly over our service functions; that is, we do not have licenses like those held by teachers, social workers, and nurses, and our knowledge and skills are widely shared across a host of other fields. "Delineating the boundaries of sociological knowledge and methods is an extremely difficult task. But I contend that we either 'stake our claim' or we lose it all," she writes (263).

If Iutcovich is correct even in part in this expression of the major challenge, it is likely that sociological practice has already "lost it all." Globalization and the Information Age have transformed the meanings basic to developing a profession. Social analysis and interpretation as well as intervention are practiced worldwide today through a wide variety of social sciences and sociotechnical engineering fields. No monopoly of practice and no monopoly of knowledge and skills are achievable, I suspect.

Her second challenge, that of developing state licensure requirements by providing clear delineations of our areas of specialization, and of obtaining public accreditation for training programs in those areas, is more easily met.

Progress has been slow but is in fact being made in this regard. Modes of accreditation have been developed. Two or three universities have secured degree-program accreditation through the resulting procedures, and others will follow. Most noteworthy has been the work of the Commission of Applied and Clinical Sociology. Some movement toward unification of the associations representing practice has been achieved; for example, a "Unity Conference" was held for the first time, in August 2000, by joint cooperation between the Sociological Practice Association and the Society for Applied Sociology.

Her third challenge, how to unify basic and applied work, is the subject of Chapters 2 and 3 of this book.

Publicizing and marketing sociological practice is the fourth of the challenges identified by Iutcovich. The field lacks substantial press coverage, and its usefulness is not widely acknowledged. This generalization has validity, but it is not at all clear how this need to be marketed can or should be met in the near future. The applied associations are very small and weak, precious as they are in other respects. The American Sociological Association remains tied to the interests of the anti-applied academics situated at the most prestigious university graduate centers. Evaluators had some success during the 1990s in marketing their specialty, and their American Evaluation Association has grown significantly in numbers and public prestige. It is very multidisciplinary in nature, however. There exists no identifiable engine with which to drive the machine of marketing.

The final challenge set forth by Iutcovich is that of keeping sociologists affiliated with the profession of sociology (which she notes does not yet actually exist). I have alluded in every chapter of this little book to the dilemma of disidentificaction. This process of moving away from identification with the field is swiftest at the baccalaureate level, less swift but very evident at the master's level, and increasingly common among doctoral graduates. Nonacademic job holders the world over come to identify with the fields of work they enter rather than with sociology. A person who graduates from law school and enters public administration rather than practicing law does not persist in presenting herself as an attorney, for example. Sociologists entering the federal civil service become data analysts, program planners, demographers, and program evaluators, and within a few years of service they often drop any disciplinary identification altogether.

As severe as these challenges may seem, there are counterforces of many kinds. The associations are emerging with new training, employment, and dissemination capabilities. Their meetings are beginning to become more magnetic—to blend new knowledge exchange with sociability and entertainment, for instance. The applied degree programs are increasing their alignment with the associations. There is a possibility of unification of the associations themselves. International, national, and regional academic associations are making increasing room for sessions and activity subsystems for practitioners.

Internet communications are a powerful and positive tool for developing sociological practice. Each association has an ever-improving Web site with impressive sets of links. Data sets and retrieval services are increasingly abundant. Publications will soon move primarily through the Internet instead of print. Email and listservs are already connecting practitioners worldwide with great speed and accuracy.

The central quest in sociology during the American era from 1920 to 1970 was to become respectable academically and politically. Many traces of this quest are still retained in the field, but the twenty-first century will most likely be preoccupied with questions of globalization and the reintegration of societies around profound changes in occupational and other social structures. Sociological practice will play an increasingly important part on the stage of these transformations, even as practitioners grope toward definitions of their own situations.

REFERENCE

Iutcovich, J. M. 1997. Sociology at a crossroads: The challenges of the new millennium. In *Directions in Applied Sociology: Presidential Addresses of the Society for Applied Sociology*, edited by S. F. Steele and J. M. Iutcovich, 253–74. Arnold, Md.: Society for Applied Sociology.

Selected Bibliography in Sociological Practice and Applied Sociology

Aiken, L. H., and D. Mechanic. 1986. *Applications of Social Science to Clinical Medicine and Health Policy*. New Brunswick, N.J.: Rutgers University Press.

Becker, H. 1966. Whose side are we on? *Social Problems* 14 (Winter): 239–47.

Bird, C. E., P. Conrad, and A. M. Fremont, eds. 2000. *Handbook of Medical Sociology*. Upper Saddle River, N.J.: Prentice Hall.

Cernea, M. M., ed. 1991. *Putting People First: Sociological Variables in Rural Development*. New York: Oxford University Press [for the World Bank].

Darling, R. B. 2000. *Clinical Sociology*. Norwell, Calif.: Kluwer Academic Publishers.

Hawdon, J., and C. Mobley. 2001. Applied sociology: What skills are important? *Social Insight* 6: 7–11.

Holt, D. H. 1990. *Management: Principles and Practices*. Englewood Cliffs, N.J.: Prentice-Hall.

Hougland, Jr., J. G. 2001. Education reform and the public: Public attitudes and public policy questions arising from the first decade of the Kentucky education reform act. *Journal of Applied Sociology* 18, no. 1: 175–88.

Larson, C. J. 1993. *Pure and Applied Sociological Theory: Problems and Issues*. Ft. Worth, Tex.: Harcourt Brace Jovanovich.

Larson, C. J., and G. R. Garrett. 1996. *Crime, Justice, and Society*. Dix Hills, N.Y.: General Hall.

Lawless, J. L., and R. L. Fox. 2001. Political participation of the urban poor. *Social Problems* 48, no. 3: 362–410.

Miller, D. C., and W. H. Form. 1980. *Industrial Sociology: Work in Organizational Life*. 3d ed. New York: Harper & Row.

Plunkett, L. C., and R. Fournier. 1991. *Participative Management: Implementing Empowerment*. New York: John Wiley & Sons.

Robinette, P. D. 2000. Mediation and minority members of academe. *Sociological Practice: A Journal of Clinical and Applied Sociology* 2, no. 3: 221–34.

Rossi, P. H., H. E. Freeman, and M. W. Lipsey. 1999. *Evaluation: A Systematic Approach*. 6th ed.. Thousand Oaks, Calif.: Sage Publications.

Rothman, R. A. 1987. *Working: Sociological Perspectives*. Englewood Cliffs, N.J.: Prentice-Hall.

Schutt, R. K. 1999. *Investigating the Social World: The Process and Practice of Research*. 2d ed. Thousand Oaks, Calif.: Pine Forge Press.

Sullivan, T. J. 1992. *Applied Sociology: Research and Critical Thinking*. New York: Macmillan.

Steele, S. F., and J. M. Iutcovich, eds. 1997. *Directions in Applied Sociology: Presidential Addresses of the Society for Applied Sociology*. Arnold, Md.: Society for Applied Sociology.

Steele, S. F., A. M. Scarisbrick-Hauser, and W. J. Hauser. 1999. *Solution-Centered Sociology: Addressing Problems through Applied Sociology*. Thousand Oaks, Calif.: Sage Publications.

Stephens, W. R., Jr. 1999. *Careers in Sociology*. 2d ed. Boston: Allyn & Bacon.

Strauss, R., ed. 1994. *Using Sociology*. Dix Hills, N.Y.: General Hall.

Swann, A. L. 1984. *The Practice of Clinical Sociology and Sociotherapy*. Cambridge, Mass.: Schenkman Publishing.

Ward, L. F. 1906. *Applied Sociology: A Treatise on the Conscious Improvement of Society*. Boston: Ginn.

Index

About the Author

ROBERT A. DENTLER is Professor Emeritus of Sociology at the University of Massachusetts in Boston. He has authored or co-authored thirteen books and one hundred articles in sociology and education.